Casenote® *Legal Briefs*

PROFESSIONAL RESPONSIBILITY

Keyed to Courses Using

Martyn and Fox's
Traversing the Ethical Minefield:
Problems, Law, and Professional Responsibility

Third Edition

Wolters Kluwer

Law & Business

About Wolters Kluwer Law & Business

Wolters Kluwer Law & Business is a leading global provider of intelligent information and digital solutions for legal and business professionals in key specialty areas, and respected educational resources for professors and law students. Wolters Kluwer Law & Business connects legal and business professionals as well as those in the education market with timely, specialized authoritative content and information-enabled solutions to support success through productivity, accuracy and mobility.

Serving customers worldwide, Wolters Kluwer Law & Business products include those under the Aspen Publishers, CCH, Kluwer Law International, Loislaw, Best Case, ftwilliam.com and MediRegs family of products.

CCH products have been a trusted resource since 1913, and are highly regarded resources for legal, securities, antitrust and trade regulation, government contracting, banking, pension, payroll, employment and labor, and healthcare reimbursement and compliance professionals.

Aspen Publishers products provide essential information to attorneys, business professionals and law students. Written by preeminent authorities, the product line offers analytical and practical information in a range of specialty practice areas from securities law and intellectual property to mergers and acquisitions and pension/benefits. Aspen's trusted legal education resources provide professors and students with high-quality, up-to-date and effective resources for successful instruction and study in all areas of the law.

Kluwer Law International products provide the global business community with reliable international legal information in English. Legal practitioners, corporate counsel and business executives around the world rely on Kluwer Law journals, looseleafs, books, and electronic products for comprehensive information in many areas of international legal practice.

Loislaw is a comprehensive online legal research product providing legal content to law firm practitioners of various specializations. Loislaw provides attorneys with the ability to quickly and efficiently find the necessary legal information they need, when and where they need it, by facilitating access to primary law as well as state-specific law, records, forms and treatises.

Best Case Solutions is the leading bankruptcy software product to the bankruptcy industry. It provides software and workflow tools to flawlessly streamline petition preparation and the electronic filing process, while timely incorporating ever-changing court requirements.

ftwilliam.com offers employee benefits professionals the highest quality plan documents (retirement, welfare and non-qualified) and government forms (5500/PBGC, 1099 and IRS) software at highly competitive prices.

MediRegs products provide integrated health care compliance content and software solutions for professionals in healthcare, higher education and life sciences, including professionals in accounting, law and consulting.

Wolters Kluwer Law & Business, a division of Wolters Kluwer, is head-quartered in New York. Wolters Kluwer is a market-leading global information services company focused on professionals.

Format for the Casenote® Legal Brief

Nature of Case: This section identifies the form of action (e.g., breach of contract, negligence, battery), the type of proceeding (e.g., demurrer, appeal from trial court's jury instructions), or the relief sought (e.g., damages, injunction, criminal sanctions).

Fact Summary: This is included to refresh your memory and can be used as a quick reminder of the facts.

Rule of Law: Summarizes the general principle of law that the case illustrates. It may be used for instant recall of the court's holding and for classroom discussion or home review.

Facts: This section contains all relevant facts of the case, including the contentions of the parties and the lower court holdings. It is written in a logical order to give the student a clear understanding of the case. The plaintiff and defendant are identified by their proper names throughout and are always labeled with a (P) or (D).

Party ID: Quick identification of the relationship between the parties.

Concurrence/Dissent: All concurrences and dissents are briefed whenever they are included by the casebook editor.

Analysis: This last paragraph gives you a broad understanding of where the case "fits in" with other cases in the section of the book and with the entire course. It is a hornbook-style discussion indicating whether the case is a majority or minority opinion and comparing the principal case with other cases in the casebook. It may also provide analysis from restatements, uniform codes, and law review articles. The analysis will prove to be invaluable to classroom discussion.

Issue: The issue is a concise question that brings out the essence of the opinion as it relates to the section of the casebook in which the case appears. Both substantive and procedural issues are included if relevant to the decision.

Holding and Decision: This section offers a clear and in-depth discussion of the rule of the case and the court's rationale. It is written in easy-to-understand language and answers the issue presented by applying the law to the facts of the case. When relevant, it includes a thorough discussion of the exceptions to the case as listed by the court, any major cites to the other cases on point, and the names of the judges who wrote the decisions.

Quicknotes: Conveniently defines legal terms found in the case and summarizes the nature of any statutes, codes, or rules referred to in the text.

Palsgraf v. Long Island R.R. Co.

Injured bystander (P) v. Railroad company (D)

N.Y. Ct. App., 248 N.Y. 339, 162 N.E. 99 (1928).

NATURE OF CASE: Appeal from judgment affirming verdict for plaintiff seeking damages for personal injury.

FACT SUMMARY: Helen Palsgraf (P) was injured on R.R.'s (D) train platform when R.R.'s (D) guard helped a passenger aboard a moving train, causing his package to fall on the tracks. The package contained fireworks which exploded, creating a shock that tipped a scale onto Palsgraf (P).

🏛 RULE OF LAW
The risk reasonably to be perceived defines the duty to be obeyed.

FACTS: Helen Palsgraf (P) purchased a ticket to Rockaway Beach from R.R. (D) and was waiting on the train platform. As she waited, two men ran to catch a train that was pulling out from the platform. The first man jumped aboard, but the second man, who appeared as if he might fall, was helped aboard by the guard on the train who had kept the door open so they could jump aboard. A guard on the platform also helped by pushing him onto the train. The man was carrying a package wrapped in newspaper. In the process, the man dropped his package, which fell on the tracks. The package contained fireworks and exploded. The shock of the explosion was apparently of great enough strength to tip over some scales at the other end of the platform, which fell on Palsgraf (P) and injured her. A jury awarded her damages, and R.R. (D) appealed.

ISSUE: Does the risk reasonably to be perceived define the duty to be obeyed?

HOLDING AND DECISION: (Cardozo, C.J.) Yes. The risk reasonably to be perceived defines the duty to be obeyed. If there is no foreseeable hazard to the injured party as the result of a seemingly innocent act, the act does not become a tort because it happened to be a wrong as to another. If the wrong was not willful, the plaintiff must show that the act as to her had such great and apparent possibilities of danger as to entitle her to protection. Negligence in the abstract is not enough upon which to base liability. Negligence is a relative concept, evolving out of the common law doctrine of trespass on the case. To establish liability, the defendant must owe a legal duty of reasonable care to the injured party. A cause of action in tort will lie where harm,

though unintended, could have been averted or avoided by observance of such a duty. The scope of the duty is limited by the range of danger that a reasonable person could foresee. In this case, there was nothing to suggest from the appearance of the parcel or otherwise that the parcel contained fireworks. The guard could not reasonably have had any warning of a threat to Palsgraf (P), and R.R. (D) therefore cannot be held liable. Judgment is reversed in favor of R.R. (D).

DISSENT: (Andrews, J.) The concept that there is no negligence unless R.R. (D) owes a legal duty to take care as to Palsgraf (P) herself is too narrow. Everyone owes to the world at large the duty of refraining from those acts that may unreasonably threaten the safety of others. If the guard's action was negligent as to those nearby, it was also negligent as to those outside what might be termed the "danger zone." For Palsgraf (P) to recover, R.R.'s (D) negligence must have been the proximate cause of her injury, a question of fact for the jury.

▶ ANALYSIS
The majority defined the limit of the defendant's liability in terms of the danger that a reasonable person in defendant's situation would have perceived. The dissent argued that the limitation should not be placed on liability, but rather on damages. Judge Andrews suggested that only injuries that would not have happened but for R.R.'s (D) negligence should be compensable. Both the majority and dissent recognized the policy-driven need to limit liability for negligent acts, seeking, in the words of Judge Andrews, to define a framework "that will be practical and in keeping with the general understanding of mankind." The Restatement (Second) of Torts has accepted Judge Cardozo's view.

Quicknotes

FORESEEABILITY A reasonable expectation that change is the probable result of certain acts or omissions.

NEGLIGENCE Conduct falling below the standard of care that a reasonable person would demonstrate under similar conditions.

PROXIMATE CAUSE The natural sequence of events without which an injury would not have been sustained.

Wolters Kluwer Law & Business is proud to offer *Casenote® Legal Briefs*—continuing thirty years of publishing America's best-selling legal briefs.

Casenote® Legal Briefs are designed to help you save time when briefing assigned cases. Organized under convenient headings, they show you how to abstract the basic facts and holdings from the text of the actual opinions handed down by the courts. Used as part of a rigorous study regimen, they can help you spend more time analyzing and critiquing points of law than on copying bits and pieces of judicial opinions into your notebook or outline.

Casenote® Legal Briefs should never be used as a substitute for assigned casebook readings. They work best when read as a follow-up to reviewing the underlying opinions themselves. Students who try to avoid reading and digesting the judicial opinions in their casebooks or online sources will end up shortchanging themselves in the long run. The ability to absorb, critique, and restate the dynamic and complex elements of case law decisions is crucial to your success in law school and beyond. It cannot be developed vicariously.

Casenote® Legal Briefs represents but one of the many offerings in Legal Education's Study Aid Timeline, which includes:

- *Casenote® Legal Briefs*
- *Emanuel® Law Outlines*
- Emanuel® *Law in a Flash* Flash Cards
- Emanuel® *CrunchTime®* Series
- *Siegel's Essay and Multiple-Choice Questions and Answers Series*

Each of these series is designed to provide you with easy-to-understand explanations of complex points of law. Each volume offers guidance on the principles of legal analysis and, consulted regularly, will hone your ability to spot relevant issues. We have titles that will help you prepare for class, prepare for your exams, and enhance your general comprehension of the law along the way.

To find out more about Wolters Kluwer Law & Business' study aid publications, visit us online at *www.wolterskluwerlb.com* or email us at *legaledu@wolterskluwer.com*. We'll be happy to assist you.

How to Brief a Case

A. Decide on a Format and Stick to It

Structure is essential to a good brief. It enables you to arrange systematically the related parts that are scattered throughout most cases, thus making manageable and understandable what might otherwise seem to be an endless and unfathomable sea of information. There are, of course, an unlimited number of formats that can be utilized. However, it is best to find one that suits your needs and stick to it. Consistency breeds both efficiency and the security that when called upon you will know where to look in your brief for the information you are asked to give.

Any format, as long as it presents the essential elements of a case in an organized fashion, can be used. Experience, however, has led *Casenote*® *Legal Briefs* to develop and utilize the following format because of its logical flow and universal applicability.

NATURE OF CASE: This is a brief statement of the legal character and procedural status of the case (e.g., "Appeal of a burglary conviction").

There are many different alternatives open to a litigant dissatisfied with a court ruling. The key to determining which one has been used is to discover *who is asking this court for what.*

This first entry in the brief should be kept as *short as possible.* Use the court's terminology if you understand it. But since jurisdictions vary as to the titles of pleadings, the best entry is the one that addresses who wants what in this proceeding, not the one that sounds most like the court's language.

RULE OF LAW: A statement of the general principle of law that the case illustrates (e.g., "An acceptance that varies any term of the offer is considered a rejection and counteroffer").

Determining the rule of law of a case is a procedure similar to determining the issue of the case. Avoid being fooled by red herrings; there may be a few rules of law mentioned in the case excerpt, but usually only one is *the* rule with which the casebook editor is concerned. The techniques used to locate the issue, described below, may also be utilized to find the rule of law. Generally, your best guide is simply the chapter heading. It is a clue to the point the casebook editor seeks to make and should be kept in mind when reading every case in the respective section.

FACTS: A synopsis of only the essential facts of the case, i.e., those bearing upon or leading up to the issue.

The facts entry should be a short statement of the events and transactions that led one party to initiate legal proceedings against another in the first place. While some cases conveniently state the salient facts at the beginning of the decision, in other instances they will have to be culled from hiding places throughout the text, even from concurring and dissenting opinions. Some of the "facts" will often be in dispute and should be so noted. Conflicting evidence may be briefly pointed up. "Hard" facts must be included. Both must be *relevant* in order to be listed in the facts entry. It is impossible to tell what is relevant until the entire case is read, as the ultimate determination of the rights and liabilities of the parties may turn on something buried deep in the opinion.

Generally, the facts entry should not be longer than three to five *short* sentences.

It is often helpful to identify the role played by a party in a given context. For example, in a construction contract case the identification of a party as the "contractor" or "builder" alleviates the need to tell that that party was the one who was supposed to have built the house.

It is always helpful, and a good general practice, to identify the "plaintiff" and the "defendant." This may seem elementary and uncomplicated, but, especially in view of the creative editing practiced by some casebook editors, it is sometimes a difficult or even impossible task. Bear in mind that the *party presently* seeking something from this court may not be the plaintiff, and that sometimes only the cross-claim of a defendant is treated in the excerpt. Confusing or misaligning the parties can ruin your analysis and understanding of the case.

ISSUE: A statement of the general legal question answered by or illustrated in the case. For clarity, the issue is best put in the form of a question capable of a "yes" or "no" answer. In reality, the issue is simply the Rule of Law put in the form of a question (e.g., "May an offer be accepted by performance?").

The major problem presented in discerning what is *the* issue in the case is that an opinion usually purports to raise and answer several questions. However, except for rare cases, only one such question is really the issue in the case. Collateral issues not necessary to the resolution of the matter in controversy are handled by the court by language known as *"obiter dictum"* or merely *"dictum."* While dicta may be included later in the brief, they have no place under the issue heading.

To find the issue, ask *who wants what* and then go on to ask *why did that party succeed or fail in getting it.* Once this is determined, the "why" should be turned into a question.

The complexity of the issues in the cases will vary, but in all cases a single-sentence question should sum up the issue. *In a few cases,* there will be two, or even more rarely, three issues of equal importance to the resolution of the case. Each should be expressed in a single-sentence question.

Since many issues are resolved by a court in coming to a final disposition of a case, the casebook editor will reproduce the portion of the opinion containing the issue or issues most relevant to the area of law under scrutiny. A noted law professor gave this advice: "Close the book; look at the title on the cover." Chances are, if it is Property, you need not concern yourself with whether, for example, the federal government's treatment of the plaintiff's land really raises a federal question sufficient to support jurisdiction on this ground in federal court.

The same rule applies to chapter headings designating sub-areas within the subjects. They tip you off as to what the text is designed to teach. The cases are arranged in a casebook to show a progression or development of the law, so that the preceding cases may also help.

It is also most important to remember to *read the notes and questions* at the end of a case to determine what the editors wanted you to have gleaned from it.

HOLDING AND DECISION: This section should succinctly explain the rationale of the court in arriving at its decision. In capsulizing the "reasoning" of the court, it should always include an application of the general rule or rules of law to the specific facts of the case. Hidden justifications come to light in this entry: the reasons for the state of the law, the public policies, the biases and prejudices, those considerations that influence the justices' thinking and, ultimately, the outcome of the case. At the end, there should be a short indication of the disposition or procedural resolution of the case (e.g., "Decision of the trial court for Mr. Smith (P) reversed").

The foregoing format is designed to help you "digest" the reams of case material with which you will be faced in your law school career. Once mastered by practice, it will place at your fingertips the information the authors of your casebooks have sought to impart to you in case-by-case illustration and analysis.

B. Be as Economical as Possible in Briefing Cases

Once armed with a format that encourages succinctness, it is as important to be economical with regard to the time spent on the actual reading of the case as it is to be economical in the writing of the brief itself. This does not mean "skimming" a case. Rather, it means reading the case with an "eye" trained to recognize into which "section" of your brief a particular passage or line fits and having a system for quickly and precisely marking the case so that the passages fitting any one particular part of

the brief can be easily identified and brought together in a concise and accurate manner when the brief is actually written.

It is of no use to simply repeat everything in the opinion of the court; record only enough information to trigger your recollection of what the court said. Nevertheless, an accurate statement of the "law of the case," i.e., the legal principle applied to the facts, is absolutely essential to class preparation and to learning the law under the case method.

To that end, it is important to develop a "shorthand" that you can use to make marginal notations. These notations will tell you at a glance in which section of the brief you will be placing that particular passage or portion of the opinion.

Some students prefer to underline all the salient portions of the opinion (with a pencil or colored underliner marker), making marginal notations as they go along. Others prefer the color-coded method of underlining, utilizing different colors of markers to underline the salient portions of the case, each separate color being used to represent a different section of the brief. For example, blue underlining could be used for passages relating to the rule of law, yellow for those relating to the issue, and green for those relating to the holding and decision, etc. While it has its advocates, the color-coded method can be confusing and time-consuming (all that time spent on changing colored markers). Furthermore, it can interfere with the continuity and concentration many students deem essential to the reading of a case for maximum comprehension. In the end, however, it is a matter of personal preference and style. Just remember, whatever method you use, underlining must be used sparingly or its value is lost.

If you take the marginal notation route, an efficient and easy method is to go along underlining the key portions of the case and placing in the margin alongside them the following "markers" to indicate where a particular passage or line "belongs" in the brief you will write:

N   (NATURE OF CASE)
RL   (RULE OF LAW)
I   (ISSUE)
HL   (HOLDING AND DECISION, relates to the RULE OF LAW behind the decision)
HR   (HOLDING AND DECISION, gives the RATIONALE or reasoning behind the decision)
HA   (HOLDING AND DECISION, applies the general principle(s) of law to the facts of the case to arrive at the decision)

Remember that a particular passage may well contain information necessary to more than one part of your brief, in which case you simply note that in the margin. If you are using the color-coded underlining method instead of marginal notation, simply make asterisks or checks in the margin next to the passage in question in the colors that indicate the additional sections of the brief where it might be utilized.

The economy of utilizing "shorthand" in marking cases for briefing can be maintained in the actual brief writing process itself by utilizing "law student shorthand" within the brief. There are many commonly used words and phrases for which abbreviations can be substituted in your briefs (and in your class notes also). You can develop abbreviations that are personal to you and which will save you a lot of time. A reference list of briefing abbreviations can be found on page x of this book.

C. Use Both the Briefing Process and the Brief as a Learning Tool

Now that you have a format and the tools for briefing cases efficiently, the most important thing is to make the time spent in briefing profitable to you and to make the most advantageous use of the briefs you create. Of course, the briefs are invaluable for classroom reference when you are called upon to explain or analyze a particular case. However, they are also useful in reviewing for exams. A quick glance at the fact summary should bring the case to mind, and a rereading of the rule of law should enable you to go over the underlying legal concept in your mind, how it was applied in that particular case, and how it might apply in other factual settings.

As to the value to be derived from engaging in the briefing process itself, there is an immediate benefit that arises from being forced to sift through the essential facts and reasoning from the court's opinion and to succinctly express them in your own words in your brief. The process ensures that you understand the case and the point that it illustrates, and that means you will be ready to absorb further analysis and information brought forth in class. It also ensures you will have something to say when called upon in class. The briefing process helps develop a mental agility for getting to the *gist* of a case and for identifying, expounding on, and applying the legal concepts and issues found there. The briefing process is the mental process on which you must rely in taking law school examinations; it is also the mental process upon which a lawyer relies in serving his clients and in making his living.

Abbreviations for Briefs

acceptance	acp		offer	O
affirmed	aff		offeree	OE
answer	ans		offeror	OR
assumption of risk	a/r		ordinance	ord
attorney	atty		pain and suffering	p/s
beyond a reasonable doubt	b/r/d		parol evidence	p/e
bona fide purchaser	BFP		plaintiff	P
breach of contract	br/k		prima facie	p/f
cause of action	c/a		probable cause	p/c
common law	c/l		proximate cause	px/c
Constitution	Con		real property	r/p
constitutional	con		reasonable doubt	r/d
contract	K		reasonable man	r/m
contributory negligence	c/n		rebuttable presumption	rb/p
cross	x		remanded	rem
cross-complaint	x/c		res ipsa loquitur	RIL
cross-examination	x/ex		respondeat superior	r/s
cruel and unusual punishment	c/u/p		Restatement	RS
defendant	D		reversed	rev
dismissed	dis		Rule Against Perpetuities	RAP
double jeopardy	d/j		search and seizure	s/s
due process	d/p		search warrant	s/w
equal protection	e/p		self-defense	s/d
equity	eq		specific performance	s/p
evidence	ev		statute	S
exclude	exc		statute of frauds	S/F
exclusionary rule	exc/r		statute of limitations	S/L
felony	f/n		summary judgment	s/j
freedom of speech	f/s		tenancy at will	t/w
good faith	g/f		tenancy in common	t/c
habeas corpus	h/c		tenant	t
hearsay	hr		third party	TP
husband	H		third party beneficiary	TPB
injunction	inj		transferred intent	TI
in loco parentis	ILP		unconscionable	uncon
inter vivos	I/v		unconstitutional	unconst
joint tenancy	j/t		undue influence	u/e
judgment	judgt		Uniform Commercial Code	UCC
jurisdiction	jur		unilateral	uni
last clear chance	LCC		vendee	VE
long-arm statute	LAS		vendor	VR
majority view	maj		versus	v
meeting of minds	MOM		void for vagueness	VFV
minority view	min		weight of authority	w/a
Miranda rule	Mir/r		weight of the evidence	w/e
Miranda warnings	Mir/w		wife	W
negligence	neg		with	w/
notice	ntc		within	w/i
nuisance	nus		without	w/o
obligation	ob		without prejudice	w/o/p
obscene	obs		wrongful death	wr/d

Table of Cases

Note: There are no principal cases in Chapter 1 of the casebook.

CHAPTER 2

Judicial and Professional Regulation of Lawyers

Quick Reference Rules of Law

In re Application of Converse

Bar applicant (P) v. Nebraska State Bar Commission (D)

Neb. Sup. Ct., 602 N.W.2d 500 (1999).

NATURE OF CASE: Appeal from denial of application to sit for Nebraska bar exam.

FACT SUMMARY: Converse (P), a law school graduate, applied to sit for the Nebraska bar exam. The Nebraska State Bar Commission (D) held a hearing into Converse's (P) moral fitness and found he did not have the requisite fitness to practice law in Nebraska. The Nebraska State Bar Commission (D) denied Converse's (P) application and he appealed.

🏛 RULE OF LAW
A pattern of acting in a hostile and disruptive manner excludes an individual from the practice of law in the state of Nebraska.

FACTS: Converse (P), in his 40s, graduated from the University of South Dakota law school and applied to sit for the July 1998 Nebraska state bar exam. Converse's (P) law school dean certified Converse's (P) graduation but checked the box requesting that the Nebraska State Bar Commission (the Commission) (D) engage in further inquiry into Converse's (P) moral fitness. Converse (P) engaged in numerous disruptive activities while at law school, including sending complaint letters to media about professors and displaying a photograph of a nude woman's backside in his study carrel. He "appealed" an appellate advocacy course grade by writing inappropriate letters to the professor, the law school dean, the South Dakota Supreme Court, and two federal judges. Converse (P) repeatedly threatened professors, the law school dean, and other students with litigation. Converse (P) had a particular problem with the law school dean, Barry Vickrey, and publicly criticized him. He made t-shirts with a nude caricature of Vickrey on the front astride a hotdog with the slogan "Astride the Peter Principle." Converse (P) stated it meant Vickrey had been promoted beyond his competency, but he conceded it had sexual overtones as well. The Nebraska State Bar Commission (D) held a hearing inquiring into Converse's (P) moral character and found it lacking. The Commission (D) denied Converse's (P) application to sit for the Nebraska bar exam. Converse (P) appealed.

ISSUE: Does a pattern of acting in a hostile and disruptive manner exclude an individual from the practice of law in the state of Nebraska?

HOLDING AND DECISION: (Per curiam) Yes. A pattern of acting in a hostile and disruptive manner excludes an individual from the practice of law in the state of Nebraska. Converse (P) first asserts the Commission (D) erred because many of his activities were protected by the First Amendment. He argued his letters to the media, public statements, letters to the law school faculty, t-shirt, and photograph were protected by his First Amendment rights and therefore not subject to censure by the Commission (D). Converse (P) concedes in oral argument that the First Amendment does not stop further inquiry into the basis for the actions. The Commission (D) did not deny the application as a prosecution for the conduct but because it inquired into the reflection of that conduct on Converse's (P) moral character. To rule in favor of Converse (P) would end all serious inquiry into an applicant's character. Converse (P) next asserts he was not informed of the "charges" against him in the proceeding. The Commission (D) can consider a person's behavior and deny an application if it finds good and bad character in even balance. Rule 3 of the Neb. Ct. R. for Adm. of Attys demands honesty, trustworthiness, respect for others, professional courtesy, and actions in accordance with the law and Code of Professional Responsibility. Applicants who are rude, use foul language toward others, intimidate, and threaten are not acceptable counselors or advocates in the legal system. Converse (P) testified that he personally attacked others when engaged in disputes. His past actions and his admissions of abusive and disruptive behavior indicate a pattern of conduct incompatible with the practice of law. These habits would not be accepted in an attorney and cannot be countenanced in an applicant to the bar. This was not a single action or isolated incident. The Commission's (D) inquiry revealed Converse (P) to be a rude, abusive, threatening, discourteous individual who often acted outside of dispute resolution arenas to personally attack and humiliate those with whom he disagreed. Affirmed.

▶ ANALYSIS

The Supreme Court held in *In Re Snyder*, 472 U.S. 634 (1985), that a "single incident of rudeness or lack of professional courtesy" does not warrant suspension from the practice of law. Similarly, a single incident of rudeness likely would not support denial of a bar application. State bar commissions have a significant responsibility to review and affirm the educational standards, moral character, and legal ability of bar applicants. The commissions are not limited to cursory examinations confirming law school graduation and non-felon status. Converse's (P) history of degrading, threatening behavior would not be tolerated in

Continued on next page.

practicing attorneys and could not be accepted in a potential colleague.

■══■

Quicknotes

FIRST AMENDMENT RIGHTS Rights conferred by the First
Amendment to the United States Constitution prohibiting
Congress from enacting any law respecting an establish-
ment of religion, prohibiting the free exercise of religion,
abridging freedom of speech or the press, the right of
peaceful assembly and the right to petition for a redress
of grievances.

■══■

People v. Walker

State bar agency (P) v. Mentally disabled attorney (D)

2011 Colo. Discipl. LEXIS 32 (2011).

NATURE OF CASE: Attorney disciplinary action.

FACT SUMMARY: Walker (D) retained unearned client funds and abandoned multiple cases. He claimed he had a major depressive disorder causing his behavior and was now receiving treatment.

🏛 RULE OF LAW
A presumptive sanction of disbarment may be lowered due to mitigating factors and the ability to eventually resume professional duties.

FACTS: Walker (D) failed to return the unearned retainers of more than a dozen clients. He also effectively abandoned cases, including Shannon Boerger's contempt action against her ex-husband. Walker (D) was late filing Boerger's motions and then failed to appear at the hearing, which resulted in the postponement of Boerger's trial. The People (P) filed a disciplinary action against Walker (D). The presumptive sanction for the multiple violations is disbarment. Walker (D) claimed he was diagnosed with a major depressive disorder which affected his behavior. He argued the mitigating circumstances of his mental disability should lower the presumptive sanction.

ISSUE: May a presumptive sanction of disbarment be lowered due to mitigating factors and the ability to eventually resume professional duties?

HOLDING AND DECISION: (Lucero, J.) Yes. A presumptive sanction of disbarment may be lowered due to mitigating factors and the ability to eventually resume professional duties. In a disciplinary action, the Hearing Board considers the duty breached, the injury or potential injury caused, the attorney's mental state, and the aggravating and mitigating circumstances. Here, Walker (D) breached some of an attorney's most fundamental client duties. His clients suffered delays, some clients experienced financial losses when Walker (D) converted funds, and courts wasted time in a loss of judicial resources. Walker (D) conceded his conduct was knowing, but he argued the mental disability should mitigate the sanction. He demonstrated true remorse, has no prior history of misconduct, and accepted responsibility for his actions. He is unlikely to reoffend if he continues treatment and works to stay healthy. Colorado case law supports a lowering of the presumptive sanction if mitigating circumstances suggest the behavior was a result of a diagnosed mental disorder, the disorder is being treated, and the attorney is likely to resume professional obligations without a recurrence of the behavior. Walker (D) argued it may be illegal to assess sanctions after a period of disability for conduct occurring during that period of disability. The Colorado Supreme Court previously held attorneys who commit serious misconduct are not qualified to serve as members of the bar and no "reasonable modifications" can be made. The Americans with Disabilities Act does not bar the imposition of sanctions. Walker's (D) mitigating circumstances do justify the lowering of the presumptive sanction from disbarment to a period of suspension. Walker (D) is suspended for three years.

▶ ANALYSIS

Hearing Boards typically have discretion to sanction attorney misconduct at the level deemed appropriate. Some egregious behavior presumes a sanction of disbarment because the attorney cannot justify or rehabilitate the behavior. A physical or chemical dependency disorder may mitigate the sanction but the disorder generally must be treatable and under control.

■■■

Quicknotes

DISBARMENT The administrative penalty levied against an attorney for a breach of professional conduct that effectively revokes the license to practice law.

SANCTIONS A penalty imposed in order to ensure compliance with a statute or regulation.

■■■

Kentucky Bar Association v. Helmers

Attorney disciplinary agency (P) v. Attorney (D)

353 S.W.3d 599 (Ky. 2011).

NATURE OF CASE: Review of attorney disciplinary action and recommended sanction.

FACT SUMMARY: Helmers (D) misled numerous clients about the nature and amount of a settlement. He also participated in financial improprieties with respect to the settlement funds.

🏛 RULE OF LAW
An attorney acting pursuant to the direction of a supervising attorney remains responsible for his own compliance with professional rules of responsibility.

FACTS: David L. Helmers (D) began as a clerk and continued as an associate at the law firm of Gallion, Baker, and Bray. He worked almost exclusively under William Gallion's supervision on dozens of actions related to clients' use of the diet drug Fen-Phen. Helmers (D) was often the primary contact for clients and opposing counsel. The court ordered mediation and Helmers (D) attended the mediation with Gallion. Helmers (D) signed the final settlement agreement and he was assigned the task of meeting with clients to review the settlement terms, get their approval, and negotiate their acceptance of a lesser amount even than that assigned to their individual claims by the firm. One of the clients learned the true settlement amount was significantly higher than that represented by Helmers (D), so Gallion authorized a second distribution to clients. Helmers (D) met with the clients again to explain the second distribution and to request authority to distribute escrowed funds to charities. One such charity was an organization for which Gallion partners were paid to serve on the board. Most of the attorneys with whom Helmers (D) worked have been disbarred for their conduct in the Fen-Phen litigation. The Kentucky Bar Association (P) charged Helmers (D) with multiple violations of multiple Rules of Professional Conduct. The Trial Commissioner determined Helmers (D) violated Rules One, Two, Three, Four, Six, and Seven. He recommended Helmers (D) be suspended for five years. The Board (P) voted to hear Helmers's (D) case de novo; determined he violated Rules One, Two, Three, Four, Six and Seven; and recommended he be disbarred.

ISSUE: Is an attorney acting pursuant to the direction of a supervising attorney responsible for his own compliance with professional rules of responsibility?

HOLDING AND DECISION: (Minton, Jr., J.) Yes. An attorney acting pursuant to the direction of a supervising attorney remains responsible for his own compliance with professional rules of responsibility. Helmers (D) had no prior disciplinary action and was a young law student when he began working with Gallion. He may have been impressionable and led astray by more experienced attorneys. Helmers (D), however, directly and personally deceived his clients with egregious injury to them. It did not require a sophisticated understanding of the ethical rules to understand his conduct was wrong. Helmers (D) is guilty of violating the ethical rules of professional conduct and is permanently disbarred from practice in the Commonwealth. All concur.

▶ ANALYSIS

An attorney's youth, inexperience, or naivete are no excuse for violating the professional rules of responsibility. Recognition of misconduct does not require a sophisticated understanding of ethical rules or years of litigation experience. Each attorney is responsible for his own conduct and ethical boundaries.

■━■

Quicknotes

DISBARMENT The administrative penalty levied against an attorney for a breach of professional conduct that effectively revokes the license to practice law.

ETHICS Of or relating to moral action, conduct, motive or character; professionally right or befitting; conforming to professional standards of conduct.

■━■

Beginning the Client-Lawyer Relationship

Quick Reference Rules of Law

Bothwell v. Republic Tobacco Co.

Inmate (P) v. Tobacco companies (D)

912 F. Supp. 1221 (D. Neb. 1995).

NATURE OF CASE: Motion for vacation of order of appointment as counsel.

FACT SUMMARY: Metcalf brought a motion for vacation of the court's order appointing her to represent Bothwell (P) on the basis that the federal court does not have the authority to compel attorneys to represent indigent clients in civil suits.

🏛 RULE OF LAW
Federal courts have inherent authority to compel unwilling attorneys to accept representation of indigent clients in civil cases if a client's indigence is the principal reason for rejecting the representation.

FACTS: Bothwell (P), an inmate at Hastings Correctional Center, submitted a request to proceed in forma pauperis, a civil complaint, and a motion for appointment of counsel. The court provisionally granted the request to proceed in forma pauperis, and ordered the complaint to be filed. Bothwell (P) alleged that he switched from smoking manufactured cigarettes to rolling his own cigarettes because he believed they were safer since the loose tobacco packages did not contain any warning labels. He later learned that he suffered from emphysema, heart disease, and other bronchial and respiratory diseases. He learned that the loose tobacco products were in fact stronger than the factory-manufactured cigarettes. Bothwell (P) filed a complaint asserting breach of implied warranty of fitness and strict liability claims. The court granted his request for appointment of counsel and eventually appointed Metcalf. Metcalf brought a motion asking for reconsideration and vacation of the order appointing her to represent Bothwell (P).

ISSUE: Do federal courts have inherent authority to compel unwilling attorneys to accept representation of indigent clients in civil cases?

HOLDING AND DECISION: (Piester, J.) Yes. Federal courts have inherent authority to compel unwilling attorneys to accept representation of indigent clients in civil cases if a client's indigence is the principal reason for rejecting the representation. Metcalf argued that a federal court does not have jurisdiction to require an attorney to take a civil case for no consideration. An extensive review of the authority and commentary with respect to this issue supports the contrary result. The court's inherent power to compel representation of indigent clients is based on two purposes: (1) to ensure fair and just adjudication and (2) to maintain the integrity and viability of the civil justice system. While a plaintiff does not have a constitutional right to counsel in a civil suit, an attorney may still be required to ensure a fair and just proceeding and result. Adequate legal representation is necessary for both parties to a dispute in order to ensure the viability of the adversarial process. Where lack of representation is the result of the client's free choice, the justice system is not offended. However, if the party cannot obtain counsel solely because of his indigence, then the underlying principles of fairness and equality are violated. Based on these principles the court concludes that (1) it has the inherent authority to utilize those "instruments" at its disposal necessary to ensure a fair and just result; (2) attorneys are a necessary component in ensuring such results; (3) indigent clients do not have sufficient access to legal representation; and (4) this lack of access may affect the fairness and reliability of the adversarial process. Thus, if indigence is the main reason for unequal access to the civil justice system, the federal court has inherent authority to compel an unwilling attorney to represent an indigent client in order to ensure a fair and just adjudication. Motion granted.

▶ ANALYSIS

While the court recognizes that the right to counsel exists in civil cases for indigent clients, it nevertheless granted Metcalf's motion for removal on the basis that it was the lack of marketability of Bothwell's (P) claims, not his indigence, that prevented him from obtaining counsel. The marketability analysis requires the court to first consider, in deciding whether to appoint counsel, whether there is a realistically available market of attorneys practicing in the area relating to the plaintiff's claims. If there is such a market, the next step is whether the plaintiff has sufficient access to that market. If both these questions are answered in the affirmative, the court must then examine whether feasible fee arrangements are available. Lastly, the court must determine whether the rejection of the client's representation was based on his indigence. Here, Bothwell (P) satisfied the first three prongs of the analysis; however, the court concluded that the rejection of his claims was not due to his indigence, but rather to the high costs of litigating against tobacco companies, thereby making his case unmarketable.

■■■

Quicknotes

IMPLIED WARRANTY OF FITNESS An implied promise made by a merchant in a contract for the sale of goods that

Continued on next page.

such goods are suitable for the purpose for which they are purchased.

IN FORMA PAUPERIS Permission to proceed with litigation without incurring fees or costs.

STRICT LIABILITY Liability for all injuries proximately caused by a party's conducting certain inherently dangerous activities without regard to negligence or fault.

■━■

Togstad v. Vesely, Otto, Miller & Keefe

Paralysis victim (P) v. Law firm (D)

Minn. Sup. Ct., 291 N.W.2d 686 (1980).

NATURE OF CASE: Appeal of award of damages for legal malpractice.

FACT SUMMARY: Ms. Togstad (P) successfully sued Miller (D) of Vesely, Otto, Miller & Keefe (D) for legal malpractice, even though she had not formally retained him.

🏛 RULE OF LAW
A retainer is not required for an attorney-client relationship that may give rise to a malpractice claim to exist.

FACTS: Ms. Togstad (P) was rendered paralyzed after a medical procedure. Fourteen months later, Ms. Togstad (P) consulted with Miller (D) of Vesely, Otto, Miller & Keefe (D) regarding a possible malpractice action. After an initial consultation, Miller (D) informed Ms. Togstad (P) that he did not think she had a case, but that he would talk to his partners. Miller (D) never called back. After Minnesota's two-year statute of limitations on medical malpractice had expired, the Togstads (P) brought a legal malpractice action against Miller (D) for giving them erroneous advice and not advising them of the two-year statute. A jury found Miller (D) to have committed malpractice and awarded over $600,000 in damages. Miller (D) and his firm (D) appealed.

ISSUE: Is a retainer required for an attorney-client relationship that may give rise to a malpractice claim to exist?

HOLDING AND DECISION: (Per curiam) No. A retainer is not required for an attorney-client relationship that may give rise to a malpractice claim to exist. The first element in a malpractice claim is the existence of an attorney-client relationship. The crux of this relationship is the provision of advice by the attorney that he either knows or should know will be followed by the person to whom he provides the advice. This does not require actual retention. Here, Ms. Togstad (P) sought and obtained legal advice from Miller (D). It was entirely reasonable for Miller (D) to have expected the Togstads (P) to have followed his advice, which is exactly what they did. As a result, for purposes of a malpractice action, an attorney-client relationship between the Togstads (P) and Miller (D) existed. Affirmed.

▶ ANALYSIS

It is unclear as to whether the attorney-client relationship is defined by contract or tort theory. Appellate courts around the nation have gone both ways on this issue, on a variety of grounds. The court here recognized this diversity of opinion but did not indicate its preference for the one theory over the other. The court believed the contract and tort analyses for this case to be so similar that they did not need to be distinguished.

■■■

Quicknotes

ATTORNEY-CLIENT PRIVILEGE A doctrine precluding the admission into evidence of confidential communications between an attorney and his client made in the course of obtaining professional assistance.

RETAINER Compensation paid in advance for professional services.

■■■

CHAPTER 4

Control and Communication

Quick Reference Rules of Law

Machado v. Statewide Grievance Committee

Disciplined attorney (P) v. State disciplinary body (D)

Conn App. Ct., 890 A.2d 622 (2006).

NATURE OF CASE: Appeal from dismissal of appeal of disciplinary reprimand.

FACT SUMMARY: The Statewide Grievance Committee (D) disciplined Arthur D. Machado (P) for his violation of two Professional Rules of Conduct. Machado (P) appealed the reprimand, but the trial court dismissed the appeal.

🏛 RULE OF LAW
An attorney must keep his or her client reasonably informed of the status of the representation.

FACTS: In January 2000, Arthur D. Machado (P) met with Scott V. Adams while Adams was incarcerated. Adams intended to file bankruptcy. Adams retained Machado (P) for the bankruptcy proceedings and instructed Machado (P) to communicate with Kendra Cihocki because of his limited means of communication as a prisoner. Cihocki delivered an $850 retainer check to Machado (P) and instructed Machado (P) to release a sales tax lien on property she and Adams jointly owned. Machado (P) did so and used up the retainer funds. Cihocki then picked up the Adams file and retained new counsel. In August 2000, Machado (P) decided to close his office and he let go all his employees. In March 2001, Machado's (P) office lease expired. Adams claimed he attempted to contact Machado (P) during that time, but he did not receive return calls or letters. Machado (P) did nothing further about Adams's bankruptcy. In March 2002, Adams filed a complaint with the Statewide Grievance Committee (the Committee) (D) for Machado's (P) failure to keep him informed about the status of his bankruptcy. The Committee (D) determined Machado (P) violated Professional Rules of Conduct 1.2(a) and 1.4(a) and ordered Machado (P) reprimanded. Machado (P) appealed to the trial court, which dismissed his appeal. Machado (P) appealed the trial court's dismissal.

ISSUE: Must an attorney keep his or her client reasonably informed of the status of the representation?

HOLDING AND DECISION: (Gruendel, J.) Yes. An attorney must keep his or her client reasonably informed of the status of the representation. Machado (P) defended his actions by stating he had kept Cihocki, Adams's agent, informed of the representation status and was then terminated by Cihocki. He also considered the tax liens to be part of the eventual bankruptcy estate issues. The Committee (D) determined Cihocki ceased to be Adams's agent when she changed the nature of the representation from bankruptcy to release of the tax liens.

Machado (P) conceded he should have prepared a new engagement letter for the tax liens representation. Machado (P) was obligated to keep Adams informed of the change in representation as well as the status of his bankruptcy proceedings. His failure to keep Adams informed occurred prior to Cihocki picking up the file from Machado's (P) office, so Machado's (P) defense that he was terminated fails. Finally, Machado's (P) scienter is not considered because he violated the Rules even if he was acting in good faith. Affirmed.

▶ ANALYSIS

Machado (P) erred when he did not obtain his client's informed consent about the change in the nature of the representation or the termination of his representation for the bankruptcy action. An attorney's professional responsibility requires that she or he consult with clients about decisions, options, and strategies before and after action is required. The client has the right to determine the course of the representation so long as that course stays within the bounds of law and ethics.

■=■

Quicknotes

BANKRUPTCY A legal proceeding whereby a debtor, who is unable to pay his debts as they become due, is relieved of his obligation to pay his creditors either by liquidation and distribution of his remaining assets or through reorganization and payment from future income.

SCIENTER Knowledge of certain facts; often refers to "guilty knowledge," which implicates liability.

■=■

Antioch Litigation Trust v. McDermott Will & Emery LLP

Trustee for bankrupt company (P) v. Corporate law firm (D)

738 F. Supp. 2d 758 (S.D. Ohio 2010).

NATURE OF CASE: Motion to dismiss in bankruptcy malpractice action.

FACT SUMMARY: McDermott Will & Emery LLP (MWE) (D) served as corporate counsel for The Antioch Company (Antioch). During its representation on tax and Employee Retirement Income Security Act (ERISA) issues, it failed to advise the board with respect to self-dealing and fairness. MWE (D) also advised the Morgans about methods to retain control, which was not in the best interests of the corporation. Antioch filed for reorganization under Chapter 11 bankruptcy.

🏛 RULE OF LAW
A malpractice claim requires (1) an attorney-client relationship; (2) a professional duty arising from that relationship; (3) breach of the duty; (4) proximate cause; and (5) damages.

FACTS: McDermott Will & Emery LLP (MWE) (D) served as corporate counsel for The Antioch Company (Antioch) from 2003 until June 5, 2008. Antioch retained MWE (D) to provide legal advice related to Employee Retirement Income Security Act (ERISA) and tax issues connected with the employee stock ownership plan (ESOP). An MWE (D) partner crafted and consummated a Tender Offer, which greatly benefitted Antioch board members CEO Lee Morgan and his daughter Asha Morgan Moran (collectively, "the Morgans"). The Morgans owned the controlling shares while four of the other board members owned significant shares. The Morgans owned 80 percent of the shares outside the ESOP. The entire board was subject to a conflict of interest, but MWE (D) failed to advise the board the Tender Offer, as an ERISA-prohibited transaction, had to be fair to Antioch as well as the shareholders or was voidable. The Tender Offer resulted in Antioch taking on massive debt. Employees left and Antioch fell further into distress. Antioch hired a consultant to find an outside buyer, but the Morgans wanted to retain control of the company. MWE (D) advised the Morgans on retaining their own financial advisor to explore alternatives to selling to an outside buyer. The company was in the final stages of an auction sale to an outside buyer, when the ESOP Trustee replaced the board to halt the sale and allow the Morgans more time to accomplish their own deal. The ESOP Trustee replaced the board with the Morgans and an acquaintance. The next day, the new board fired MWE (D). Antioch did not sell or refinance and entered bankruptcy proceedings. The Trustee for the bankruptcy Antioch Liti-

gation Trust (the "Trustee") (P) filed a malpractice action against MWE (D). MWE (D) moved to dismiss.

ISSUE: Does a malpractice claim require (1) an attorney-client relationship; (2) a professional duty arising from that relationship; (3) breach of the duty; (4) proximate cause; and (5) damages?

HOLDING AND DECISION: (Black, J.) Yes. A malpractice claim requires (1) an attorney-client relationship; (2) a professional duty arising from that relationship; (3) breach of the duty; (4) proximate cause; and (5) damages. MWE (D) had a duty to advise its client, Antioch, the Tender Offer had to be approved by a disinterested majority of board members after full disclosure or it was a voidable transaction. If the Tender Offer was voided, the ESOP would not be a qualified plan and Antioch would owe substantial taxes. The directors on the board had a fiduciary duty to Antioch to ensure fair dealing. MWE (D) did not appropriately advise its client. The Trustee (P) stated a claim. The Trustee (P) also supported a claim the Tender Offer violated ERISA and burdened the company with bankruptcy-inducing debt. The Trustee (P) also properly stated a claim MWE (D) aided and abetted the Morgans' breaches of fiduciary duty to Antioch. MWE (D) advised the Morgans and aided their own self-interest. MWE (D) failed to advise the board it had claims for breach of fiduciary duty against the Morgans or claims of professional negligence against financial advisors. The board never received opinions of the fairness of the share price with respect to the corporation. Finally, MWE (D) failed to advise the board to stop the dual track of looking for an outside purchase while also permitting the Morgans to craft alternatives to retain control. The Trust (P) conceded MWE (D) had no duty to provide "business advice" to Antioch, but it did have a duty to advise the board against self-dealing. The Trustee (P) can bring any claim Antioch could have brought. The motion to dismiss is denied.

▶ ANALYSIS

Attorneys representing entities must be clear about the identity of his or her clients. The attorney may communicate solely with one individual within the corporation, but the entity itself is the client and the attorney's responsibility is to the client. The attorney's duty and loyalty is to the entity and not any one individual employed by the entity.

■■■

Continued on next page.

Quicknotes

ATTORNEY-CLIENT RELATIONSHIP The confidential relationship established when a lawyer enters into employment with a client.

CONFLICT OF INTEREST Refers to ethical problems that arise, or may be anticipated to arise, between an attorney and his client if the interests of the attorney, another client or a third-party conflict with those of the present client.

FAIR DEALING An implied warranty that the parties will deal honestly in the satisfaction of their obligations and without intent to defraud.

FIDUCIARY DUTY A legal obligation to act for the benefit of another, including subordinating one's personal interests to that of the other person.

SELF-DEALING Transaction in which a fiduciary uses property of another, held by virtue of the confidential relationship, for personal gain.

dePape v. Trinity Health Systems, Inc.

Canadian physician (P) v. U.S. employer (D)

242 F. Supp. 2d 585 (N.D. Iowa 2003).

NATURE OF CASE: Breach of contract and legal malpractice.

FACT SUMMARY: Trinity Health Systems, Inc. (Trinity) D) contracted with Canadian physician Gregory dePape (P) to bring dePape (P) to Iowa to act as a family physician. Trinity (D) hired Blumenfeld, Kaplan & Sandweiss, P.C. (D) law firm to work on dePape's (P) immigration issues and Blumenfeld (D) agreed to act on behalf of Trinity (D) and dePape (P). Blumenfeld (D) never communicated with dePape (P), however, until he was literally preparing to cross the border. dePape (P) was denied entry by U.S. Immigration and Naturalization Service (INS) officials and he was unable to start his new job and life in Iowa.

🏛 RULE OF LAW
An attorney is obligated to consider his client's best interests as determined through conversations with and decisions made by the client.

FACTS: Trinity Health Systems, Inc. (Trinity) (D) wanted to bring a family physician to the medically under-served community of Fort Dodge, Iowa. Trinity (D) contracted with Canadian physician Gregory dePape (P). DePape (P) agreed to move to Fort Dodge for the five-year contract term with the intention of remaining throughout his medical career as Fort Dodge's family physician. Trinity (D) hired St. Louis law firm Blumenfeld, Kaplan & Sandweiss, P.C. (D) to work through dePape's (P) immigration issues. Blumenfeld (D) conferenced with Trinity (D) but failed to notify dePape (P) of the conference or its content afterwards. Blumenfeld (D) then drafted an engagement letter stating it would act as the attorney for Trinity (D) and dePape (P) but only sent the letter to Trinity (D). Blumenfeld (D) determined dePape (P) would not qualify for the H-1B visa, which is the most common visa used to bring foreign physicians to work in the United States, because dePape (P) had not successfully completed the United States Medical Licensing Examination (USMLE). Blumenfeld (D) never communicated with dePape (P), so failed to inform him that he could complete the USMLEs in six to eight months and then qualify for the H-1B visa. DePape (P) mistakenly believed it took two years to complete the USMLEs, so had never begun the process. DePape (P) could not qualify for the TN visa as a family physician, so Blumenfeld (D) developed a new title and job description for dePape (P) as a Physician Consultant serving as a community health care consultant. Blumenfeld (D) did not notify Trinity (D) or dePape (P) of their actions. Over the next months, dePape (P) quit his job, packed his home,

and he and his fiancée prepared to move permanently to Iowa. Trinity (D) told dePape (P) to cross the border in Buffalo, New York, because Blumenfeld (D) had a relationship with an Immigration and Naturalization Service (INS) officer there. The morning of the crossing, Blumenfeld's (D) local New York counsel met with dePape (P) for the first time for about 20 minutes. This was the first time dePape (P) learned of the new job title and description and his inability to practice as a family physician under the TN visa. DePape (P) was advised to inform the INS that he was planning to serve as the Physician Consultant. DePape (P) then attempted to cross the border, was questioned by the INS official, told the truth about his intention to practice as a family physician, and was denied entry to the United States. He telephoned Trinity (D) and a representative told him to wait 30 minutes and try to cross again as a visitor. He did so and the INS officials recognized him. They detained him and his fiancée, called dePape (P) a "liar," and he felt generally humiliated. Blumenfeld (D) never contacted dePape (P) again. DePape (P) and his fiancée paid their own way back to their former city where he eventually opened his own practice. DePape (P) filed this lawsuit against Trinity (D) for breach of contract and Blumenfeld (D) for legal malpractice.

ISSUE: Is an attorney obligated to consider his client's best interests as determined through conversations with and decisions made by the client?

HOLDING AND DECISION: (Bennett, C.J.) Yes. An attorney is obligated to consider his client's best interests as determined through conversations with and decisions made by the client. The claims asserted against Trinity (D) are dismissed. DePape's (P) claim against Blumenfeld (D) for failure to pursue the H-1B visa fails because no evidence exists that dePape (P) would have taken the USMLEs even if Blumenfeld (D) advised him to do so. Negligence evidence is usually presented through expert testimony unless the negligence is so egregious that a layperson recognizes it as such. The negligence here is so obvious that expert testimony is unnecessary. Attorneys have professional and ethical obligations to keep their clients informed and advised so the clients can make educated decisions. Blumenfeld (D) advertises its own dedication to client contact but completely failed to communicate at all with dePape (P). Blumenfeld (D), at the least, should have sent the engagement letter to dePape (P), informed him of the visa issues, and advised him as to dealing with the INS other than the proffered advice to lie to the U.S. officials to gain entry. Blumenfeld (D) breached

Continued on next page.

its duty to communicate with dePape (P). Proof of proximate causation in a legal malpractice case requires the plaintiff to prove that damage would not have occurred but for the defendant's negligence. Here, dePape (P) would have found employment in Canada but for Blumenfeld's (D) failure to advise and communicate. The result was that dePape (P) lost $203,736.20 in U.S. dollars of income. Further, dePape (P) can recover for emotional distress because Blumenfeld's (D) negligence placed him directly in harm. Blumenfeld (D), through local counsel, advised dePape (P) to lie to INS officials which directly led to the U.S. denying dePape (P) entry. dePape (P) may therefore recover his lost income plus $75,000 in emotional distress damages. The facts of this case certainly justify the award of punitive damages also but the court finds that dePape (P) did not adequately plead facts to place Blumenfeld (D) on notice that punitive damages could be sought. Plaintiff's claims dismissed.

▶ ANALYSIS

A client has the right to reasonably direct his representation in legal matters but cannot do so unless he receives proper advice. The attorney cannot meet his obligation to focus on the client's best interests when the client is not fully advised of his options and given the opportunity to provide input. Communication between attorney and client is vital to a strong, working relationship and required by the professional rules of responsibility.

Quicknotes

BREACH OF CONTRACT Unlawful failure by a party to perform its obligations pursuant to contract.

CAUSATION The aggregate effect of preceding events that bring about a tortious result; the causal connection between the actions of a tortfeasor and the injury that follows.

EMOTIONAL DISTRESS Extreme personal suffering which results from another's conduct and for which damages may be sought.

LEGAL MALPRACTICE Conduct on the part of an attorney falling below that demonstrated by other attorneys of ordinary skill and competency under the circumstances, resulting in damages.

NEGLIGENCE Conduct falling below the standard of care that a reasonable person would demonstrate under similar conditions.

PUNITIVE DAMAGES Damages exceeding the actual injury suffered for the purposes of punishment of the defendant, deterrence of the wrongful behavior or comfort to the plaintiff.

Maples v. Thomas

Convicted murderer (P) v. [Party not identified in casebook] (D)

132 S. Ct. 912 (2012).

NATURE OF CASE: Appeal from denial of federal habeas corpus relief.

FACT SUMMARY: Maples (P) was convicted of two counts of capital murder and sentenced to death. Volunteer attorneys for Maples' post-conviction relief abandoned him and he subsequently missed an appeal deadline.

🏛 RULE OF LAW
A client cannot be faulted for failing to act on his own behalf when he has no notice his attorneys of record are no longer representing his interests.

FACTS: An Alabama jury convicted Maples (P) of two counts of capital murder and recommended the death penalty. Maples (P) was represented by two court-appointed attorneys, only one of whom had tried a capital murder case and neither of which had experience with the penalty phase of a capital case. The trial court accepted the jury's recommendation and sentenced Maples (P) to death. The Alabama Court of Criminal Appeals and the Alabama Supreme Court affirmed the convictions and sentence. Two New York attorneys, Munanka and Ingan-Housz, from the Sullivan & Cromwell law firm volunteered to represent Maples in post-conviction proceedings. The attorneys associated with local counsel, John Butler. Mr. Butler informed Munanka and Ingan-Housz he could not deal with the substantive issues in the case but would appear only to permit the two to enter pro hac vice. The attorneys agreed. Maples filed a petition for post-conviction relief. Seven months later, Munanka and Ingan-Housz each left Sullivan & Cromwell for other positions, but failed to inform the Court or Maples (P). Nearly one year later, the court, without holding a hearing, denied Maples (P) petition and mailed copies of the order to the three attorneys of record. The notices arrived at the Sullivan & Cromwell New York offices, but were not forwarded to another attorney. Instead, the mail clerk returned the unopened envelopes to the Court stamped "Return to Sender—Attempted, Unknown" on Munanka's and a handwritten "Return to Sender—Left Firm" on Ingan-Housz's. The court clerk took no further action upon receiving the returned notices. Butler did receive the Order, but assumed Munana or Ingan-Housz would act on it and he did nothing. Maples had 42 days from the date of the denial to file a notice of appeal, but the time expired with no notice filed. One month after the deadline, the State attorney sent a letter directly to Maples (P) informing him of an impending deadline to file a federal habeas petition. The State did not copy any of Maples' attorneys

of record. Maples (P) contacted his mother who contacted Sullivan & Cromwell. Three Sullivan & Cromwell attorneys filed a motion asking the Court to reissue its order, thus starting the appeal timeline anew. The Court refused, noting Maples (P) still had attorneys of record and the three new Sullivan & Cromwell attorneys had not entered appearances in the case. Maples (P) sought federal habeas corpus relief, but the State argued he forfeited his claims when he failed to file a timely appeal. The District Court agreed with the State Maples had procedurally defaulted on his ineffective assistance of counsel claims and a divided panel of the Eleventh Circuit affirmed.

ISSUE: Can a client be faulted for failing to act on his own behalf when he has no notice his attorneys of record are no longer representing his interests?

HOLDING AND DECISION: (Ginsberg, J.) No. A client cannot be faulted for failing to act on his own behalf when he has no notice his attorneys of record are no longer representing his interests. The Court does not disturb the general rule that an agent is bound by the mistakes of his principal. A petitioner's post-conviction attorney is the petitioner's agent. The negligence of the agent does not establish cause to overcome procedural default. It is markedly different, however, when the agent abandons the petitioner with no notice and thus occasions the default. The attorney is not acting as the petitioner's representative in that instance. As Justice Alito previously noted, a litigant cannot be held responsible for the attorney's conduct when the attorney is not operating as the agent in any meaningful sense of that word. Maples (P) only had three attorneys of record and no notice none of the attorneys were acting on his behalf. The State argued Sullivan & Cromwell represented Maples throughout the process, but Munanka and Ingan-Housz severed their agency relationship nine months before the Court entered its order. The record is cloudy on what role other Sullivan & Cromwell attorneys may have played. None of the three who filed the late motion to reconsider were properly entered in the case or had the legal authority to act on Maples' (P) behalf. Butler never attempted to represent Maples (P) at all. The attorneys should have informed Maples (P) of their departure so he could file the appeal himself or obtain new representation. There was cause to excuse Maples' (P) procedural default. These were extraordinary circumstances quite beyond Maples' (P) control.

CONCURRENCE: (Alito, J.) Maples (P) was effectively deprived of legal representation because (1) his

Continued on next page.

counsel of record left their firm; (2) the attorneys' new employment precluded continued representation of Maples; (3) the attorneys failed to notify Maples; (4) the attorneys failed to withdraw; (5) the firm the attorneys left failed to monitor the case; (6) the firm's mail department failed to forward the notices to another firm member or the former attorneys; (7) the clerk's office took no action when the envelopes returned unopened; and (8) local counsel had limited conception of the role he was to play. Petitioner's attorneys effectively abandoned Maples (P) and that is "cause" sufficient to overcome his procedural default.

▶ *ANALYSIS*

An attorney has a communication obligation with his client whether the client is an entity or individual, paying or pro bono client. Once the attorney-client relationship is established, the attorney owes a duty of care to that client, which includes a requirement for ongoing communication. Local counsel also should clarify with retaining counsel the extent of the communication he or she should have with the joint client. An attorney can never err with too much communication to the client.

■■■■

Quicknotes

DUTY OF CARE A principle of negligence requiring an individual to act in such a manner as to avoid injury to a person to whom he or she owes a duty.

PRO BONO Services rendered without charge.

PRO HAC VICE Applicable to a specific occasion; the use or application of a condition for the limited duration of a single situation.

■■■■

Missouri v. Frye

State (P) v. Unlicensed driver (D)

132 S. Ct. 1399 (2012).

NATURE OF CASE: Certiorari review of ineffective assistance of counsel claim.

FACT SUMMARY: Frye (D) was convicted three times of driving with a revoked license and he was charged with a fourth offense. The prosecutor sent two plea offers to Frye's (D) attorney but the attorney failed to notify Frye (D) and the offers expired. Frye (D) was then charged with a fifth offense prior to pleading guilty to the fourth offense. The state trial judge sentenced him to a three-year sentence.

🏛 RULE OF LAW
The Sixth Amendment guarantees effective assistance of counsel throughout all critical stages of trial, including pretrial plea negotiations.

FACTS: In August 2007, Galin Frye (D) was charged with driving with a revoked license. He had been convicted for that offense on three prior occasions, so Missouri (P) charged Frye (D) with a Class D felony. On November 15, the prosecutor sent Frye's (D) attorney two plea offers addressing Frye (D) pleading guilty to the felony and accepting a three-year sentence and ten days "shock" time in jail or pleading guilty to a misdemeanor and serving 90 days in jail. Frye's (D) attorney did not communicate the offers to Frye (D) and the offers expired. One week prior to the preliminary hearing, Frye (D) was arrested again for driving with a revoked license. He eventually pleaded guilty to the first charge without an underlying plea agreement. The state trial court accepted his guilty plea and sentenced him to three years in prison. [Frye (D) appealed] claiming ineffective assistance of counsel. The United States Supreme Court accepted certiorari review with the companion case *Lafler v. Cooper*, 132 S. Ct. 1376 (2012).

ISSUE: Does the Sixth Amendment guarantee effective assistance of counsel throughout all critical stages of trial, including pretrial plea negotiations?

HOLDING AND DECISION: (Kennedy, J.) Yes. The Sixth Amendment guarantees effective assistance of counsel throughout all critical stages of trial, including pretrial plea negotiations. The right to effective assistance of counsel applies to certain steps before trial. *Strickland v. Washington*, 466 U.S. 668 (1984) sets forth a two-part test: (1) counsel's representation falls below an objective level of reasonableness; and (2) a reasonable possibility exists, but for counsel's errors, the proceeding results would have been different. Plea bargains have become so central to the administration of the criminal justice system that defense attorneys have Sixth Amendment responsibilities to meet the adequate assistance of counsel. Benefits to both the state and the defendant require effective assistance of counsel during plea negotiations. The American Bar Association recommends prompt communication of all plea offers. Numerous state and federal courts have adopted that standard over the last 30 years. Professional standards for attorneys also set forth that recommendation. Frye's (D) attorney did not make a meaningful attempt to communicate the plea offers to Frye (D) before they expired. Frye (D) also has to show, however, a reasonable probability the outcome would have been different. Given Frye's (D) new offense for driving without a license, it is unlikely the plea bargain would have remained in place or the state court judge would have accepted the original plea agreement. [Decision not stated in casebook excerpt.]

DISSENT: (Scalia, J.) The only difference in these cases is the fairness of the conviction in *Lafler* was established by a full trial and jury verdict while this conviction arose out of a guilty plea preceded by a voluntary and truthful admission of guilt. The fairness of the convictions is clear. The Court's sledge may require a reversal of a valid, and eminently just, conviction.

▌ *ANALYSIS*

An attorney must communicate with his client. The "fairness" of the conviction in *Frye* would not be an issue had the attorney promptly communicated the plea bargains to his client. Each attorney has an ethical obligation to prompt and ongoing communication with each client.

■=∎

Quicknotes

ASSISTANCE OF COUNSEL The right to counsel guaranteed by the Sixth Amendment to the U.S. Constitution.

PLEA BARGAIN An agreement between a prosecutor and a criminal defendant that is submitted to the court for approval, generally involves the defendant's pleading guilty to a lesser charge or count in exchange for a more lenient sentence.

■=∎

Lafler v. Cooper

Convicted assaulter (D) v. [Party not identified in casebook] (P)

132 S. Ct. 1376 (2012).

NATURE OF CASE: Certiorari review of ineffective assistance of counsel claim.

FACT SUMMARY: Lafler (D) shot and wounded Mundy, but Mundy survived. Lafler (D) was arrested and charged with multiple counts, including assault with intent to commit murder. Lafler's (D) attorney advised Lafler (D) the State could not convict on the assault count because Mundy was only shot in her lower body. Lafler (D), relying on his attorney's advice, rejected the plea offers from the prosecutor. A jury convicted him on all counts and he was sentenced to 3.5 times the number of years he would have served under the plea bargain.

RULE OF LAW

Sixth Amendment remedies should "neutralize the taint" of the constitutional violations without providing a windfall to the defendant or wasting the State's resources expended in the criminal prosecution.

FACTS: On March 25, 2003, Lafler (D) shot at Kali Mundy's head, but missed. Mundy fled, Lafler (D) pursued and continued shooting. Mundy survived several gunshot wounds to her lower body. Lafler (D) was charged with multiple offenses. The prosecution twice offered to dismiss two counts and recommend a sentence of 51 to 85 months for the remaining two in exchange for a guilty plea. Lafler (D) informed the court of his willingness to accept the offer, but then rejected the offer both times. Lafler (D) claimed his counsel advised him the state would be unable to prove intent to murder because Mundy was shot in the lower body. On the first day of trial, the prosecutor offered a significantly less favorable plea deal, which Lafler (D) rejected. A jury convicted Lafler (D) on all counts and he was sentenced to the mandatory minimum of 185 to 360 months' imprisonment. [Lafler (D) appealed].

ISSUE: Should Sixth Amendment remedies "neutralize the taint" of the constitutional violations without providing a windfall to the defendant or wasting the State's resources expended in the criminal prosecution?

HOLDING AND DECISION: (Kennedy, J.) Yes. Sixth Amendment remedies should "neutralize the taint" of the constitutional violations without providing a windfall to the defendant or wasting the State's resources expended in the criminal prosecution. Defendant may meet the two-part *Strickland* test [*Strickland v. Washington*, 466 U.S. 668 (1984)], but the question of the remedy remains. All parties agree Lafler's (D) counsel's advice with respect to assault with intent to murder was deficient performance. Lafler

(D) has shown he would have accepted the lesser sentence of the plea offer absent his counsel's deficient performance. There is a reasonable probability the trial court would have accepted the plea agreement, and, as a consequence of rejecting the offer, Lafler (D) received a sentence 3.5 times greater. The district court ordered specific performance of the original plea agreement. The proper remedy, however, is to order the State to reoffer the plea agreement. The state trial court can then determine whether to vacate the convictions and resentence Lafler (D) pursuant to the plea agreement, vacate part of the convictions, or leave the trial convictions and sentence undisturbed.

DISSENT: (Scalia, J.) The Court's remedy to reoffer the plea agreement would be a powerful remedy but for the fact the Court left the result of the acceptance of that agreement to the discretion of the trial court. The Court is camouflaging its failure to fashion a remedy. Any remedy it provides will undo the results of a fair adversarial process. Most countries forbid plea bargains in cases as serious as this because of an admirable belief the law is the law and those who break it should be punished. The United States permits plea bargaining and results in significantly lower sentences for guilty defendants. Plea bargaining is accepted because of the belief the criminal justice system would grind to a halt without it. Today, the Court elevates the plea bargain to a constitutional right. Here, even though the defendant is guilty of the offense, received the exorbitant gold standard of American justice, i.e. a criminal trial with the associated constitutional protections, and was found unanimously guilty by impartial jurors, the Court declares his conviction invalid because he was deprived of his constitutional entitlement to plea-bargain. The Court today embraces the theory the State gives each player a fair chance to beat the house and serve less time than he deserves.

▌ ANALYSIS

Effective communication between an attorney and his or her client requires the attorney to understand the basis for the communication, the effect of the communication, and the potential consequences of his or her advice. The *Lafler* decision emphasizes the importance of plea bargain communications and advice in the United States criminal justice system. The case was less about the "fairness" of the criminal conviction and more about the fairness of the defendant getting improper advice from his counsel.

▬═▬

Continued on next page.

Quicknotes

ASSISTANCE OF COUNSEL   The right to counsel guaranteed by the Sixth Amendment to the U.S. Constitution.

PLEA BARGAIN   An agreement between a prosecutor and a criminal defendant that is submitted to the court for approval, generally involves the defendant's pleading guilty to a lesser charge or count in exchange for a more lenient sentence.

Competence

Quick Reference Rules of Law

Nebraska ex rel. Counsel for Discipline of the Nebraska Supreme Court v. Orr

State disciplinary agency (P) v. General practice attorney (D)

Neb. Sup. Ct., 759 N.W.2d 702 (2009).

NATURE OF CASE: Attorney disciplinary action.

FACT SUMMARY: Orr (D) thought he was competent to practice in the specialized area of franchise law. His inexperience and unfamiliarity with franchise law resulted in serious deficiencies in his client's franchise disclosure documents.

 RULE OF LAW
An attorney must be competent in the area of law in which he practices.

FACTS: Orr (D) was a private practice attorney in Nebraska with limited franchising experience. He previously reviewed franchisee agreements, but had no experience representing franchisors. Orr (D) nevertheless agreed to represent Steve Sickler and Cathy Mettenbrink in the franchising of their coffee shop business, Barista's Daily Grind. Orr (D) prepared franchising documents, including a Federal Trade Commission (FTC) disclosure statement, and Barista's was franchised numerous times in multiple states. Orr (D) did contact another attorney for trademark and copyright issues and that attorney told Orr (D) franchising was a specialized area of the law. Orr (D) felt comfortable he was competent to continue his representation and believed franchising was merely a matter of contract-drafting. After a few years, Sickler and Mettenbrink were involved in litigation with Colorado franchisees and a dispute with an Iowa franchisee. Orr (D) paid for another firm to provide a second opinion of his FTC disclosures and the other firm revealed serious deficiencies in the franchise documents. Orr's (D) associate, Holbrook, handled the litigation, but eventually referred Sickler and Mettenbrink to an attorney specializing in franchise law. The franchise attorney noted "major" deficiencies in the franchise documents. Orr (D) and his firm withdrew from representation. The Nebraska disciplinary agency filed several charges against Orr (D) for violation of Nebraska Rules of Professional Conduct requiring a lawyer to provide competent representation. The court-appointed referee determined Orr (D) violated Rules 1.1 and 8.4(a).

ISSUE: Must an attorney be competent in the area of law in which he practices?

HOLDING AND DECISION: (Per curiam) Yes. An attorney must be competent in the area of law in which he practices. The disciplinary proceeding is a trial de novo on the record and the charges must be supported by clear and convincing evidence. The referee's findings are final and conclusive and provide clear and convincing evidence

Orr (D) violated Rules 1.1 and 8.4(a). The purpose of disciplinary action is not necessarily to punish the attorney but determine whether it is in the public's interest for the attorney to continue to practice. Here, the referee found a number of mitigating factors in Orr's (D) favor. He practiced for over 40 years with no prior complaints, he was an active leader in his community, and served the legal community well. Orr's (D) misconduct involved one client and was an isolated occurrence. Further, Orr (D) did not knowingly engage in misconduct, but believed he was competent to practice in the area of franchise law. He should have been aware, however, that he was not competent to represent franchisors. He should have at least done the research to become competent. A general practitioner should not take on unfamiliar areas of the law unless he is willing to do the research to become competent in the relevant area. If the general practitioner enters into a field in which he is not competent, and makes mistakes that demonstrate incompetence, discipline must be imposed. [Discipline not stated in casebook].

ANALYSIS

No attorney graduates law school completely versed in any area of the law, which is why attorneys spend time researching and learning particular areas to become competent to practice. Some areas of the law such as trademark or franchise law require specialized knowledge beyond that typically held by general practice attorneys. The good intentions of an attorney practicing outside her knowledge base does not erase mistakes she makes because she is unfamiliar with a practice area and can result in serious harm to a client's case or business.

Quicknotes

TRIAL DE NOVO A new trial conducted as if there had not previously been a trial.

Bayview Loan Servicing, LLC v. Law Firm of Richard M. Squire & Associates, LLC

Creditor client (P) v. Law firm (D)

2010 U.S. Dist. LEXIS 132108 (E.D. Penn. 2010).

NATURE OF CASE: Malpractice claim.

FACT SUMMARY: Bayview Loan Servicing, LLC (Bayview) (P) claimed Law Firm of Richard M. Squire & Associates, LLC (Squire Firm) (D) breached its fiduciary duty to Bayview (P) and committed negligent malpractice when Squire Firm (D) failed to file a petition within the six months statute of limitations. The failure to file the petition meant Bayview (P) lost its opportunity to recover a deficiency judgment against its debtor.

🏛 RULE OF LAW
A plaintiff must prove the action, or inaction, of the attorney was not solely in the plaintiff's best interests and resulted in damages to the plaintiff.

FACTS: Law Firm of Richard M. Squire & Associates, LLC (Squire Firm) (D) represented Bayview Loan Servicing, LLC (Bayview) (P) in a foreclosure action. Bayview (P) directed Squire Firm (D) to proceed to collect the deficiency of $377,499.00, which statutorily required Squire Firm (D) to file a petition to fix the fair value of the property within six months of the foreclosure sale. Squire Firm (D) missed the filing deadline, allegedly informed the court to mark the judgment satisfied, and did not disclose the missed deadline to Bayview (P). Bayview (P) filed a petition for damages against Squire Firm (D) and the firm employee M. Troy Freedman (Freedman) (D). Squire Firm (D) and Freedman (D) filed motions to dismiss for failure to state a cause of action.

ISSUE: Must a plaintiff prove the action, or inaction, of the attorney was not solely in the plaintiff's best interests and resulted in damages to the plaintiff?

HOLDING AND DECISION: (Yohn, J.) Yes. A plaintiff must prove the action, or inaction, of the attorney was not solely in the plaintiff's best interests and resulted in damages to the plaintiff. Defendants (D) argued Bayview (P) failed to specifically allege it would have won the deficiency litigation, thus it failed to state claim for negligent malpractice. A Pennsylvania legal malpractice claim sounding in negligence requires plaintiffs to prove (1) employment of attorney; (2) attorney's failure to exercise ordinary skill and knowledge; and (3) such negligence was the proximate cause of plaintiffs' damages. Bayview (P) alleged all necessary elements of the legal malpractice claim because it claims it suffered damages arising out of Squire Firm's (D) "careless, negligent and reckless conduct" in failing to file the necessary petition to fix fair value. A Pennsylvania disloyalty claim may be maintained for breach of an attorney's fiduciary duty to his client. This is a breach of loyalty rather than a breach of duty of care. The plaintiffs must prove (1) defendant negligently or intentionally failed to act in good faith and solely for plaintiffs' benefit in the matter for which he was engaged; (2) plaintiffs suffered injury; and (3) the injuries were brought about by defendant's failure to act. Bayview (P) does not allege the failure to file the petition was intentional or due to divided loyalties. It does, however, allege the subsequent cover-up attempts constituted a failure to act solely in the plaintiffs' interest. Bayview (P) will have to prove the subsequent acts directly led to the damages, but it has properly pled its claim. Bayview (P) met its burden to plead a breach of contract claim. Defendants (D) argued Bayview's (P) negligent supervision claim failed because there is no allegation Freedman (D) acted outside his employment. That is not necessary and there can be concurrent liability for employer and employee. Finally, Bayview (P) sought punitive damages, which requires plaintiff to plead defendant acted outrageously due to evil motive or reckless indifference, subjectively appreciated the harm, and acted or failed to act in conscious disregard of that harm. Bayview (P) alleged conscious wrongdoing in this case. The original mistake may only constitute negligence, which is insufficient for punitive damages, but the subsequent actions support a plausible claim for punitive damages. [Decision not included in casebook].

▶ ANALYSIS

A missed deadline may result in damages to a client and the attorney can be found responsible for the consequences. A missed deadline followed by a cover-up and an attempt to avoid responsibility can lead to breach of fiduciary duty claims and punitive damages. An attorney can limit his liability for mistakes by immediately reporting them.

■=■

Quicknotes

BREACH OF FIDUCIARY DUTY The failure of a fiduciary to observe the standard of care exercised by professionals of similar education and experience.

PUNITIVE DAMAGES Damages exceeding the actual injury suffered for the purposes of punishment of the defendant, deterrence of the wrongful behavior or comfort to the plaintiff.

■=■

Greycas, Inc. v. Proud

Lender (P) v. Attorney (D)

826 F.2d 1560 (7th Cir. 1987), *cert. denied*, 484 U.S. 1043 (1988).

NATURE OF CASE: Appeal of award of damages against an attorney under professional liability principles.

FACT SUMMARY: Greycas, Inc. (P) contended that Proud's (D) misrepresentations in his capacity as attorney to Crawford, a party adverse to Greycas (P), were actionable.

🏛 RULE OF LAW
An attorney may be professionally liable to one adverse to his client.

FACTS: Crawford was in dire need of capital for his farm business. He approached Greycas, Inc. (P) about a loan, offering his farm machinery as collateral. Upon Greycas's (P) demand, Crawford retained Proud (D), an attorney (and Crawford's brother-in-law), to draft a letter to the effect that he had performed a records search and was satisfied that the machinery had no prior security interests. This Proud (D) did, even though he had in fact conducted no search, and the machinery was subject to a prior security interest. Based on Proud's (D) assertions, Greycas (P) loaned over $1 million to Crawford. The following year, Crawford defaulted and committed suicide. Greycas (P), discovering that it had no security interest of any value, sued Proud (D). A district court, sitting in diversity, entered a judgment of $833,760 in Greycas's (P) favor. Proud (D) appealed, contending he owed no duty to Greycas (P).

ISSUE: May an attorney be professionally liable to one adverse to his client?

HOLDING AND DECISION: (Posner, J.) Yes. An attorney may be professionally liable to one adverse to his client. Courts long ago jettisoned concepts of contractual privity as requirements for liability, replacing them with more general concepts of duty. When the facts of a particular case are sufficient for the finding of such a duty, the adversarial or non-adversarial relationship of the parties is of little moment. In this particular case, Proud (D) made certain misrepresentations to Greycas (P), either intentionally or negligently, or both. The misrepresentations were intended to induce reliance and did in fact induce reliance on the part of Greycas (P), to Greycas's (P) detriment. Whether one considers this to be a case of professional liability or negligent misrepresentation or fraud does not matter. The bottom line is that, under the facts here, Proud (D) owed a duty of care to Greycas (P), which he breached. Affirmed.

▶ ANALYSIS

The court here never quite made it clear to the reader whether it reached its conclusion based on professional liability principles or more general principles of misrepresentation. The court essentially admitted this to be the case, but disclaimed any importance thereto. This is not necessarily so, however. Whether the award was based on malpractice or misrepresentation could impact on the availability of insurance indemnification, as well as whether various professional rules of conduct could be implicated.

Quicknotes

FRAUD A false representation of facts with the intent that another will rely on the misrepresentation to his detriment.

PRIVITY Commonality of rights or interests between parties.

SECURITY INTEREST An interest in property that may be sold upon a default in payment of the debt.

Cruze v. Hudler

Property owners (P) v. Scam artist (D)

Ore. Ct. App. 267 P.3d 176 (2011), *modified*, Ore. Ct. App. 274 P.3d 858 (2012).

NATURE OF CASE: Appeal from summary judgment in fraud action.

FACT SUMMARY: Cruze (P) met with Hudler (D) and Markley (D) multiple times about development projects and business ventures. Hudler (D) convinced Cruze (P) to invest in multiple companies. Markley (D) drafted legal documents to accomplish the investment. Cruze (P) alleged the companies were all a part of a complicated Ponzi-scheme.

🏛 RULE OF LAW
An attorney may be liable to third parties when his conduct or his support of his client's tortious conduct results in damages suffered by the third parties.

FACTS: Tyrone and Jacqueline Cruze (collectively, Cruze) (P) owned development property in Oregon. Martin L. Hudler (D) claimed to be interested in purchasing the property with his business partner Charles R. Markley (D). Hudler and Markley (D) marketed themselves and their alleged development projects to Cruze (P) over a period of time. Hudler (D) stated Markley (D) was a "successful lawyer" and a partner in a top law firm in Portland. Cruze (P) agreed to form a joint venture with Hudler (D) and Markley's (D) company, Bridgeport Communities, LLC (Bridgeport). Hudler (D) also approached Cruze (P) about investing in another Hudler (D) and Markley (D) company, Covenant Partners, LLC (Covenant). Markley (D) prepared a First Amended and Restated Operating Agreement of Covenant Partners, LLC and Hudley (D) presented it to Cruze (P). Cruze (P) agreed to purchase half of Bridgeport's interest in Covenant for $513,149 and loan an additional $3.3 million to yet another of Hudler (D) and Markley's (D) companies, Keycom. According to plaintiffs, Cruze (P) relied on financial statements provided by Hudler (D) and the investment information contained within the legal documents drafted by Markley (D). Cruze (P) later discovered numerous financial inaccuracies and subsequently filed complaints against Hudler (D) and Markley (D). It appeared the entire business scheme was a "Ponzi-scheme" with Hudler (D) and Markley (D) paying old investors from new investors' funds. Hudler (D) moved for summary judgment, which motion the court denied. Markley (D) also moved for summary judgment, which motion the court granted because there was no evidence Markley (D) himself made misrepresentations to Cruze (P).

ISSUE: Will an attorney be liable to third parties when his conduct or his support of his client's tortious conduct results in damages suffered by the third parties?

HOLDING AND DECISION: (Schuman, J.) Yes. An attorney may be liable to third parties when his conduct or his support of his client's tortious conduct results in damages suffered by the third parties. In a common-law fraud claim based on misrepresentation, the plaintiff must prove the defendant made a misrepresentation intended to deceive the plaintiff or with reckless disregard for the truth. Cruze (P) attributed the bulk of the misrepresentations to Hudler (D), but argued Markley (D) affirmatively misrepresented contribution figures in legal documents. Markley (D) argued he merely repeated the information he was provided by his client. In addition to the written misrepresentations, however, evidence was presented that Markley (D) had actual knowledge Hudler (D) was "stealing" from others. A reasonable trier of fact could conclude Markley (D) made affirmative misrepresentations hoping Cruze (P) would agree to invest in the client's business. Cruze (P) next claimed Markley (D) provided substantial assistance to Hudler (D) in the effort to fraudulently induce plaintiffs to invest. A person assisting another in committing a tort may be liable to a third party if he acts in concert with the tortious conduct of another, knows the conduct constitutes a breach of duty and gives substantial assistance, or gives substantial assistance to the tortious conduct and his own separate conduct constitutes a breach of duty to the third person. Markley (D) argued Cruze (P) had to prove he was acting outside the scope of his lawyer-client privilege with Covenant. Markley (D) was wearing two hats here—that of owner and that of attorney. An attorney is not privileged to commit common-law fraud. The trial court erred in granting Markley (D) summary judgment on joint liability for Hudler's (D) misrepresentations. Issues of fact also existed as to whether Markley (D) was a manager of securities seller Bridgeport and his liability for securities law violations. Further, Markley (D) could be liable for financial elder abuse based on his allegedly wrongful taking of money from a vulnerable person. Finally, the court should reconsider its refusal to permit Cruze (P) to amend the petition to include counts for Oregon Racketeer Influenced and Corrupt Organizations Act (ORICO). Plaintiffs allege multiple violations of ORICO based on Hudler (D) and Markley (D) fraudulently obtaining Cruze (P) signatures on numerous legal documents. Reversed and remanded.

▶ ANALYSIS

An attorney's conduct in support of another's tortious actions is not privileged merely by the existence of an attorney-client relationship with the tortfeasor. An attorney

Continued on next page.

always has an affirmative duty to comply with ethical rules and refrain from knowingly participating in or supporting misconduct. Zealous advocacy of a client's goals cannot extend into deliberate damage inflicted on non-clients.

■═■

Quicknotes

MISREPRESENTATION A statement or conduct by one party to another that constitutes a false representation of fact.

■═■

Confidentiality

Quick Reference Rules of Law

Matter of Anonymous

Disciplinary commission (P) v. Sanctioned attorney (D)

Ind. Sup. Ct., 654 N.E.2d 1128 (1995).

NATURE OF CASE: Disciplinary action against an attorney.

FACT SUMMARY: In reviewing a potential client's documents, the attorney discovered a conflict and did not represent the individual. The attorney did use information from the documents in a later action against the individual.

▄ RULE OF LAW
An attorney owes a duty to a nonclient to not reveal damaging information learned in the course of consultations for potential representation.

FACTS: Mother sought to engage counsel (D) for a potential support action. She sent documents, which included financial information for the father, to the attorney. In reviewing the documents, the attorney discovered a joint judgment against the mother and father for the child's medical bills. The judgment was in favor of the welfare department, another client of the attorney's, and counsel learned the debt had not been paid by either the mother or the father. Counsel informed mother of the conflict and sent her documents to another attorney at her request. The attorney then filed a collection action on behalf of the welfare department against the father based on the information from the mother that the father was about to inherit a substantial sum and was gainfully employed. Father joined mother as a co-defendant and counsel did not withdraw.

ISSUE: Does an attorney owe a duty to a nonclient to not reveal damaging information learned in the course of consultations for potential representation?

HOLDING AND DECISION: (Per curiam) Yes. An attorney owes a duty to a nonclient to not reveal damaging information learned in the course of consultations for potential representation. The attorney here violated Indiana Professional Conduct Rules 1.6(a), 1.8(b) and 1.16(a)(1). Counsel revealed information relating to mother's representation without her consent, which violates Rule 1.6(a). He used that information to her disadvantage without her consent, which violates Rule 1.8(b). He then failed to withdraw when continued representation of the welfare department against the mother violated the Rules, which violated Rule 1.16(a)(1). The misconduct is mitigated by the fact that the information was publicly available, counsel did not request mother to sign an engagement letter, pay a retainer, or pay a fee. Further, counsel did not represent mother upon learning of the conflict. Counsel appears to have no selfish or sinister motives. The conduct, however, erodes the integrity of the profession as well as causes harm to the individuals involved. The agreed sanction of a private reprimand is accepted.

▶ ANALYSIS

An attorney's fiduciary responsibilities arise even during preliminary consultations if the attorney engages in substantive review or discussion of the potential legal issues. Individuals approach attorneys with sensitive information and the belief that the attorney will protect that information along with the client's trust. The ethics rules support that belief when requiring attorneys to abide by fiduciary duties. An attorney may be unable or unwilling to accept representation of a potential client, but may not disclose the content of that individual's communications, particularly where the disclosure will prejudice the individual.

■■■

Quicknotes

FIDUCIARY DUTY A legal obligation to act for the benefit of another, including subordinating one's personal interests to that of the other person.

■■■

Perez v. Kirk & Carrigan

Truck driver (P) v. Attorneys (D)

Tex. Ct. App., 822 S.W.2d 261 (1991).

NATURE OF CASE: Appeal from summary judgment in action for breach of fiduciary duty, infliction of emotional distress, and consumer protection violations.

FACT SUMMARY: After Perez's (P) truck accident claimed the lives of twenty-one children, lawyers Kirk & Carrigan (D) disseminated to the district attorney's office the confidential statements he made to them, resulting in Perez's (P) indictment.

RULE OF LAW
A lawyer may breach his fiduciary duty to his client by disclosing an unprivileged statement after wrongfully representing that it would be kept confidential.

FACTS: Perez (P), a truck driver for the Valley Coca-Cola Bottling Company, was in a traffic accident which resulted in the deaths of twenty-one children. Kirk & Carrigan (D), lawyers hired to represent Valley Coca-Cola Bottling Company, visited Perez (P) the day after the accident in the hospital and told him they were his lawyers too. Perez (P) gave a sworn statement to Kirk & Carrigan (D) with the understanding that the statement would be kept confidential. Soon thereafter, Kirk & Carrigan (D) voluntarily disclosed Perez's (P) statement to the district attorney's office under threat of subpoena. The district attorney's office obtained an indictment for involuntary manslaughter against Perez (P) based upon the statement. Perez (P) brought an action for breach of fiduciary duty against Kirk & Carrigan (D). Kirk & Carrigan (D) moved for summary judgment on the ground that the attorney-client privilege did not apply to Perez's (P) statement. The trial court granted summary judgment, and Perez (P) appealed.

ISSUE: Does a lawyer breach his fiduciary duty to maintain his client's confidences by disclosing an unprivileged statement after representing that it would be kept confidential?

HOLDING AND DECISION: (Dorsey, J.) Yes. A lawyer breaches his fiduciary duty to maintain his client's confidences by disclosing an unprivileged statement after representing that it would be kept confidential. Perez's (P) allegation here that Kirk & Carrigan (D) breached their fiduciary duty owed to him when they voluntarily disseminated his statement to the district attorney's office was a valid claim for damages for the emotional distress and mental anguish he suffered after being indicted. Once an attorney-client relationship arose between Kirk & Carrigan

(D) and Perez (P), Kirk & Carrigan (D) had a fiduciary and ethical duty not to disseminate statements Perez (P) made to them in confidence, regardless of whether the statements were privileged or not. The relationship between attorney and client requires absolute and perfect candor, openness and honesty, and the absence of any concealment or deception. Perez (P) has made a valid claim for damages. Reversed and remanded.

ANALYSIS

It is important to note that much information that is ethically protected will not be privileged. However, virtually all information considered privileged under the Rules of Evidence will also be ethically protected. A lawyer whom a court orders to reveal information that is ethically protected but not privileged under the Rules of Evidence will be required to reveal the information under pain of contempt. But if that lawyer had voluntarily revealed the same information, he or she might be guilty of a disciplinary violation for failure to protect a client's secrets or confidences, unless revelation was for one of the purposes recognized by DR 4-101 or Rule 1.6.

Quicknotes

ATTORNEY-CLIENT PRIVILEGE A doctrine precluding the admission into evidence of confidential communications between an attorney and his client made in the course of obtaining professional assistance.

FIDUCIARY DUTY A legal obligation to act for the benefit of another, including subordinating one's personal interests to that of the other person.

Hughes v. Meade

Criminal defense attorney (P) v. Judge (D)

Ky. Sup. Ct., 453 S.W.2d 538 (1970).

NATURE OF CASE: Original proceeding for writ of prohibition.

FACT SUMMARY: The Hon. N. Mitchell Meade (D) ruled Hughes (P) in contempt of court for refusing to name a client when testifying as a witness. Hughes (P) filed this action to prohibit Judge Meade (D) from enforcing the order.

🏛 RULE OF LAW
A client communication is not privileged when the attorney is merely acting as a conduit.

FACTS: Williams was on trial for the theft of an IBM typewriter. Attorney Hughes (P) was called as a witness because he had participated in the return of an IBM typewriter to the police. Hughes (P) did not represent any party at Williams's trial and was not himself a party. Hughes (P) testified that "a certain party" called him and asked if he could return an unidentified item to the police because Hughes (P) had a good relationship with the local police department. Hughes (P) contacted an officer and asked if the police would be interested in the return of stolen property and could Hughes (P) stay uninvolved. The officer agreed, so Hughes (P) contacted the "certain party" and agreed to the terms. On a Saturday morning, Hughes (P) kept his shades pulled down, heard someone place an object on his front porch, contacted the officer, and the police retrieved the wrapped package from the porch. Hughes (P) did not see the party delivering the package, did not see the package, and did not know the package's contents. When unwrapped, the package held an IBM typewriter. Hughes (P) received payment and that was the end of his involvement. On the stand, Hughes (P) was asked the name of the party who contacted him. Hughes (P) refused to answer. The Hon. N. Mitchell Meade (D) found Hughes (P) in contempt of court for his refusal to name the party. Hughes (P) filed this writ of prohibition to prohibit Judge Meade (D) from enforcing the contempt ruling.

ISSUE: Is a client communication privileged when the attorney is merely acting as a conduit?

HOLDING AND DECISION: (Clay, Commr.) No. A client communication is not privileged when the attorney is merely acting as a conduit. Hughes (P) argues the name of the client is a privileged communication not subject to disclosure. The applicable statute prohibits disclosure of client communications made to the attorney "in his professional character" absent client waiver. Client communications are not privileged, however, when the attorney is not acting in his professional capacity as a lawyer but merely acting as a conduit to deliver instruments to a third party. Here, the principal transaction was the delivery of stolen property to the police. Hughes (P) was not receiving a client communication in his professional capacity as an attorney and he was not rendering legal advice. Clients cannot use attorneys as a shield to conceal transactions involving stolen property. That goes beyond the scope of privilege and an attorney's professional duty. Writ denied.

▶ ANALYSIS

Hughes (P) had a good relationship with the police department, which is why the unnamed client contacted him. Hughes (P) did not provide legal advice and arguably provided no legal services at all. The privilege may have attached to the client's communications had Hughes (P) engaged in further investigation of the client's issue or advised the client as to his rights and obligations. Hughes's (P) desire to "stay out of it" may have resulted in the loss of privilege for his client's communications.

Quicknotes

CONTEMPT OF COURT Conduct that is intended to obstruct the court's effective administration of justice or to otherwise disrespect its authority.

WRIT OF PROHIBITION A writ issued by a superior court prohibiting a lower court from exceeding its jurisdiction or from usurping jurisdiction beyond that authorized by law.

Dean v. Dean

[Parties not identified.]

Fla. Dist. Ct. App., 607 So. 2d 494 (1992).

NATURE OF CASE: Appeal granted motion to compel testimony.

FACT SUMMARY: Husband subpoenaed an attorney to testify as to the identity of a client potentially involved in the theft of Husband's property. Attorney refused to testify, so Husband filed a motion to compel.

🏛 RULE OF LAW
The attorney-client privilege protects the identity of a client consulting an attorney regarding stolen property.

FACTS: Husband's business was burgled and the thief stole personal property and cash. An unidentified individual later contacted attorney Krischer to inquire about returning stolen property to the police. Krischer had been involved in a high-profile hit-and-run case where he refused to divulge the identity of the driver pursuant to the attorney-client privilege. The individual referenced that case in the initial phone call to Krischer. The individual and Krischer met twice and Krischer advised the individual to provide him the stolen property so he could return it to the police. The individual demanded confidentiality. An individual gave Krischer's receptionist two duffel bags, informed her Krischer would know what they were, and Krischer delivered the duffel bags to the police. He told police that they may have something to do with Husband's case. Coincidentally, the receptionist was also a client of Husband's divorce lawyer who learned about Krischer's involvement. Husband's lawyer then subpoenaed Krischer to testify about the identity of the person involved in the theft. Krischer refused, so Husband filed a motion to compel the testimony. The trial court granted the motion and Krischer appeals.

ISSUE: Does the attorney-client privilege protect the identity of a client consulting an attorney regarding stolen property?

HOLDING AND DECISION: (Farmer, J.) Yes. The attorney-client privilege protects the identity of a client consulting an attorney regarding stolen property. The individual contacted Krischer because he is an attorney, solicited and received legal advice and services regarding returning the stolen property, and insisted on confidentiality. An attorney does not have to represent a client in a legal proceeding or in court for the attorney-client privilege to apply. It also benefits the public to permit a thief to remain unidentified when the stolen property is being returned to the police. A legal service was rendered here rather than Krischer acting as a mere conduit because legal advice was given. Reversed.

▶ ANALYSIS

This case differs from *Hughes v. Meade*, Ky. Sup. Ct., 453 S.W.2d 538 (1970). Here the attorney was contacted in his position as an attorney, whereas Hughes was contacted because he had a good relationship with police officers. Also note that Krischer gave legal advice about returning the stolen property rather than simply agreeing to act as the conduit. It would have a chilling effect on attorney-client communications if clients believed attorneys would be required to disclose confidential details depending on the nature of the case. So long as legal advice and/or legal services are rendered, the attorney-client privilege applies.

■ ═ ■

Quicknotes

SUBPOENA A command issued by court to compel a witness to appear at trial.

■ ═ ■

Upjohn Co. v. United States

Audited corporation (D) v. Internal Revenue Service (P)

449 U.S. 383 (1981).

NATURE OF CASE: Review of discovery order in tax investigation.

FACT SUMMARY: The Internal Revenue Service (P), in a tax investigation of Upjohn Co. (D), sought disclosure of communications between middle- and lower-level employees and Upjohn's (D) attorneys.

🏛 RULE OF LAW
The attorney-client privilege between a corporation and its counsel extends to communications between counsel and noncontrol-level employees.

FACTS: The Internal Revenue Service (IRS) (P), in the course of a tax investigation of Upjohn Co. (D), sought disclosure of memoranda compiled by corporate attorneys during the course of their communications with nonsupervisory personnel. Upjohn (D) resisted, claiming the attorney-client privilege. The court of appeals held that the privilege applied only to communications between counsel and "control" employees, such as executives and senior management. The Supreme Court granted review.

ISSUE: Does the attorney-client privilege between a corporation and its counsel extend to communications between counsel and noncontrol-level employees?

HOLDING AND DECISION: (Rehnquist, J.) Yes. The attorney-client privilege between a corporation and its counsel extends to communications between counsel and noncontrol-level employees. The privilege exists largely because of a recognition in the law that sound legal advice depends upon the lawyer being fully informed of relevant facts; if communications between a client and his counsel were discoverable, such communication would be largely circumscribed. In the context of a corporation, the information necessary for the corporation's attorneys to properly represent the corporation will not always come from the corporation's "control group," and often the information will be in the possession of midlevel or even low-level employees. Communications between such employees and counsel may be no less necessary for proper representation, and therefore are no less deserving of confidentiality. Therefore, the privilege must be extended to all communications between counsel and corporate employees, no matter what level. Reversed.

▶ ANALYSIS

It is important to note that the attorney-client privilege protects communications only, not information. While an attorney may not be compelled to disclose what a corporate attorney communicated to him, the privilege does not bar the party seeking discovery from obtaining the information from the employee through a recognized discovery procedure such as a deposition. While it would be more convenient for the IRS (P), for example, to simply subpoena the notes taken by Upjohn's (D) attorney, the court notes that considerations of convenience do not overcome the policies served by the attorney-client privilege.

■■■

Quicknotes

ATTORNEY-CLIENT PRIVILEGE A doctrine precluding the admission into evidence of confidential communications between an attorney and his client made in the course of obtaining professional assistance.

■■■

In re Vioxx Products Liability Litigation

[Parties not identified.]

501 F. Supp. 2d 789 (E.D. La. 2007).

NATURE OF CASE: Discovery dispute in multi-district products liability case.

FACT SUMMARY: Merck claimed privilege on nearly 30,000 documents, most of which were email communications. The court appointed a Special Master to review a sample of the withheld documents and issue recommendations for the discovery process.

🏛 RULE OF LAW
Attorney-client communications not related to the request for or rendering of legal advice are not privileged communications.

FACTS: Prescription drug Vioxx was available to the public to relieve pain and inflammation. Merck withdrew Vioxx from the market in 2004 when clinical trial revealed the drug increased the likelihood of heart attacks and ischemic strokes. Plaintiffs in the subsequent multidistrict litigation (MDL) sought to discover approximately 30,000 documents from Merck for deposition preparation purposes. Merck claimed the documents were privileged attorney-client communications or work product. The court appointed Special Master Rice to review 2,000 representative documents and 600 additional documents selected by plaintiffs. Rice provided a document-by-document analysis and a 21-page report on privilege.

ISSUE: Are attorney-client communications not related to the request for or rendering of legal advice privileged communications?

HOLDING AND DECISION: (Fallon, J.) No. Attorney-client communications not related to the request for or rendering of legal advice are not privileged communications. Special Master Rice considered the primary purpose of the withheld documents. Attorney-client privilege does not apply to business communications, which can be problematic in a company structured like Merck where nearly every communication goes through the legal counsel's office for review and comment. Attorney-client privilege applies only when legal advice is the primary purpose for the communication. Merck argued the FDA's pervasive regulation of its industry rendered seemingly non-legal communications part of legal advice. It was Merck's burden to establish this on a document-by-document basis. It is accepted that Merck's responses to warning letters from the Food and Drug Administration (FDA) are the equivalent to preparation of pleadings and those documents are privileged. Limited circulation of communications seeking legal advice is classic attorney-client privilege. Email messages with the primary purpose of obtaining general business advice from a number of departments are not privileged. Forwarded emails were found to be privileged if they were forwarded by the lawyer for the purpose of rendering legal advice. Work product does not protect communications concerning non-legal things, such as news releases. Courts cannot bear the burden of document-by-document review when privilege is claimed on 30,000 documents. The sample resolution process and "packaging" of withheld documents appear to be strong solutions. A pretrial order setting forth a discovery organization method is suggested. Detailed privilege logs are also recommended.

▶ ANALYSIS

The mere existence of an attorney-client relationship does not render every communication, email, letter, or discussion privileged. Many clients retain attorneys essentially for business advice. Large corporations with active legal departments frequently provide advice or critiques on non-legal issues and communications. Clients cannot rely on the lawyer's inclusion to protect the communication from discovery.

Quicknotes

ATTORNEY-CLIENT PRIVILEGE A doctrine precluding the admission into evidence of confidential communications between an attorney and his client made in the course of obtaining professional assistance.

ATTORNEY-CLIENT RELATIONSHIP The confidential relationship established when a lawyer enters into employment with a client.

In re Pressly

Sanctioned attorney (D)

Vt. Sup. Ct., 628 A.2d 927 (1993).

NATURE OF CASE: Appeal from public sanction for disciplinary violation.

FACT SUMMARY: Vermont attorney Thomas Pressly (D) shared confidential information from his client with opposing counsel. The Professional Conduct Board recommended a public reprimand as sanction for violating the disciplinary code.

🏛 RULE OF LAW
An attorney shall not reveal the confidential communications of his client.

FACTS: Complainant engaged Vermont attorney Thomas Pressly (D) to represent her in a divorce and abuse case. She informed Pressly (D) of her estranged husband's history of physical abuse and her concern about his behavior toward their minor children. She received temporary custody of the children with supervised visitation for the father prior to the divorce agreement. The attorneys for the parties then negotiated an agreement giving the father unsupervised visitation. Complainant became increasingly concerned about father's behavior and expressed her fears to Pressly (D) who told her supervised visitation was not an option. He never filed a motion for supervised visitation. Complainant then learned from a counselor that the father may have sexually abused the nine-year-old daughter and she informed Pressly (D). She expressly asked Pressly (D) to keep this confidential from father and father's attorney until a physician could examine the daughter. Father's attorney asked Pressly (D) whether sexual abuse was an issue and Pressly (D) informed opposing counsel about complainant's suspicions. He then asked the attorney to keep that information confidential from his client. Opposing counsel wrote a letter to Pressly (D) the next day regarding the accusations and complainant learned Pressly (D) had violated her confidence. She filed this complaint and the Professional Conduct Board recommended a public reprimand for Pressly (D). He appealed.

ISSUE: May an attorney reveal the confidential communications of his client?

HOLDING AND DECISION: (Per curiam) No. An attorney shall not reveal the confidential communications of his client. Pressly (D) may not have intended to harm his client or cause her additional anguish, but he knew the information was shared in confidence and he told the opposing counsel anyway. Complainant suffered emotional distress even if her case was not adversely affected by the disclosure. Further, Pressly (D) does not claim the disclosure was necessary to protect the child. He merely felt pressed when asked by opposing counsel about sexual abuse. Pressly (D) may not have intended to disregard his client's confidence, so a suspension is too harsh, but a private reprimand is inadequate for the violation. Affirmed.

▶ ANALYSIS

Pressly (D) could have argued that his client gave him implied authority to waive confidentiality if he had shared the communications to protect the child. He admitted, however, that he just felt pressured to breach his client's confidentiality. That seems slightly absurd when opposing counsel merely asked him if sexual abuse was an issue. The attorney-client privilege is the client's and client's may waive that confidentiality. Clients can also provide an implied waiver if the communication is something that needs to be shared to move the legal system freely along. When faced with an expressly confidential communication, however, attorneys generally do not have the right to breach the client's confidence.

Quicknotes

ATTORNEY-CLIENT PRIVILEGE A doctrine precluding the admission into evidence of confidential communications between an attorney and his client made in the course of obtaining professional assistance.

IMPLIED AUTHORITY Inferred power granted, but not expressly given, to an agent to act on behalf of the principal in order to effectuate the principal's objective.

Swidler & Berlin v. United States

Law firm (P) v. Federal government (D)

524 U.S. 399 (1998).

NATURE OF CASE: Appeal from order compelling attorney production of client notes.

FACT SUMMARY: James Hamilton (P), an attorney with Swidler & Berlin (P), met with Vincent W. Foster, Jr. and took three pages of handwritten notes. Foster subsequently committed suicide. The Federal Government (D) requested production of those notes during a criminal investigation of Foster and others. Hamilton (P) objected on the basis of attorney-client privilege.

🏛 RULE OF LAW
Attorney-client privilege survives the death of the client even where the disclosure might aid a criminal investigation.

FACTS: Vincent W. Foster, Jr., Deputy White House Counsel, engaged attorney James Hamilton (P) of the law firm of Swidler & Berlin (P) for advice regarding the Federal Government's (D) Office of the Independent Counsel's investigations into Foster's role in firings at the White House Travel Office. Hamilton (P) met with Foster and took three pages of handwritten notes. The notes begin with the word "privileged." Nine days after the meeting, Foster committed suicide. The Government (D) requested the notes to advance its investigation and sought Hamilton's (P) testimony before the Grand Jury. Hamilton (P) objected on the basis of attorney-client privilege. The appeals court held the privilege did not apply posthumously, so the notes should be disclosed. Hamilton (P) appealed and the United States Supreme Court granted certiorari.

ISSUE: Does attorney-client privilege survive the death of the client even where the disclosure might aid a criminal investigation?

HOLDING AND DECISION: (Rehnquist, C.J.) Yes. Attorney-client privilege survives the death of the client even where the disclosure might aid a criminal investigation. The Government (D) advances several arguments that permitting another exception to the privilege would not chill client confidences in attorneys, but no empirical evidence exists to support the arguments. Most case law, scholarly articles, and general belief support the theory that the privilege survives the client's death. A client may not confide in an attorney knowing that the confidence might be disclosed if a later criminal or civil matter arises and the confidence became substantially important at that time although seemingly unimportant initially. Additionally, a client may wish to prohibit the disclosure of confidences even posthumously to protect his reputation,

his family, or his finances. The attorney-client privilege prohibits the production of the notes in this case. Reversed.

DISSENT: (O'Connor, J.) A client's posthumous right to confidentiality may be overridden where authorities have a compelling need for information or a criminal defendant's right to exculpatory evidence supersedes and no other method of obtaining the information is available. This would be a narrow exception where the good outweighs the harm.

▶ ANALYSIS

The attorney-client privilege is revered in the American legal system as a method of encouraging full and honest disclosures by clients to attorneys to ensure a smooth transaction or honest case. Attorneys cannot adequately fulfill their duties to their clients, opposing counsel, or the courts if they have not first received honest communications from clients. When the court orders disclosure, however, attorneys must be aware that their duty to their client may be overridden by the court's order. The attorneys here were successful in overturning the lower court's disclosure order and thus protected their client's confidentiality. Where an appeal is inappropriate or unsuccessful, attorneys must concede to the court's inherent authority to order disclosure despite the privilege or face disciplinary action.

■=■

Quicknotes

ATTORNEY-CLIENT PRIVILEGE A doctrine precluding the admission into evidence of confidential communications between an attorney and his client made in the course of obtaining professional assistance.

CERTIORARI A discretionary writ issued by a superior court to an inferior court in order to review the lower court's decisions; the Supreme Court's writ ordering such review.

■=■

Merits Incentives, LLC v. The Eighth Judicial District Court of the State of Nevada

Distributor (D) v. Trial court (D)

Nev. Sup. Ct., 262 P.3d 720 (2011).

NATURE OF CASE: Appeal from denial of motion to disqualify in breach of contract action.

FACT SUMMARY: Bumble's (P) attorney, Mowbray, received evidence from an anonymous source. Mowbray promptly notified opposing counsel, disclosed the evidence, and requested affirmation of the evidence in discovery requests. Petitioners (D) failed to object for months and then sought to disqualify Mowbray.

RULE OF LAW
An attorney who receives documents related to a case from an anonymous source must promptly notify opposing counsel or risk being in violation of ethical duties and disqualified as counsel.

FACTS: Cadeau Express, Inc. (Cadeau) (D) terminated the employment of Mohamed Issam Abi Haidar (Haidar). Cadeau (D) sued Haidar and obtained a permanent injunction prohibiting him from distributing stolen corporate information to customers, manufacturers, suppliers, or business partners. Subsequently, Cadeau (D), Merits Incentives, LLC (Merits) (D), and Ramon DeSage (D) (collectively, Petitioners) contracted with Bumble and Bumble (Bumble) (P) to distribute Bumble's (D) salon products to a Las Vegas hotel. Bumble (P) alleged Petitioners (D) distributed product to parties outside the contract and filed suit against Petitioners (D). On September 24, 2009, Bumble (P) received an anonymous package from Lebanon at its New York headquarters with directions to forward the package to its attorney, John Mowbray, in Las Vegas. On October 15, 2009, Mowbray served a supplemental NRCP 16.1 mandatory pretrial discovery disclosure (the "16.1 disclosure") on Petitioners (D). The 16.1 disclosure included a copy of the disk and the envelope in which it arrived. It identified the disk as received by Bumble (P) on September 24, 2009, from an anonymous source. Approximately one month later, Mowbray filed a second 16.1 supplemental disclosure and again included a copy of the disk. In November 2009, Mowbray filed a second request for production of documents individually requesting over 500 documents on the disk. Petitioners (D) did not object to Mowbray having the disk or its contents. In January 2010, Petitioners (D) filed a general objection to the discovery requests but still did not object to Mowbray having the disk or its contents. On January 27, 2010, Mowbray used several of the disk's documents in a deposition of Petitioners' (D) employee, but Petitioners (D) did not object. In May 2010, Petitioners (D) objected for the first time to Bumble's (P) use and possession of the disk and contents. Petitioners (D) filed a motion to dismiss Bumble's (P) case with prejudice, or alternatively, prohibit Bumble (P)

from using the misappropriated, confidential, and privileged documents and for disqualification of Bumble's (P) counsel. The trial court denied the motion and issued findings of facts in which it noted Mowbray conspicuously disclosed possession of the disk and neither Bumble (P) nor its counsel had actual knowledge of the injunction against Haidar. [Petitioners (D) appealed].

ISSUE: Must an attorney who receives documents related to a case from an anonymous source promptly notify opposing counsel or risk being in violation of ethical duties and disqualified as counsel?

HOLDING AND DECISION: (Hardesty, J.) Yes. An attorney who receives documents related to a case from an anonymous source must promptly notify opposing counsel or risk being in violation of ethical duties and disqualified as counsel. The parties here agree RPC 4.4(b) is not applicable because the disk was not inadvertently sent to Mowbray. Petitioners (D) then cite to unpersuasive case law wherein the attorney did not execute an affidavit that the discoverable material was sent anonymously. Mowbray did execute such an affidavit. He also did not take some affirmative action to obtain or solicit the evidence; it was sent anonymously. The district court appears to have applied Rule 4.4(b) by analogy, which requires the recipient attorney to notify the sender of the inadvertently received documents. The reasoning is accurate. Mowbray did promptly notify opposing counsel through the 16.1 disclosure of his receipt of the evidence from an anonymous source. He therefore fulfilled his ethical duties. He might, however, risk disqualification had he reviewed privileged documents. One document on the disk, a draft affidavit, was determined to be privileged. Disqualification is appropriate (1) if the attorney knew or should have known the material was privileged; (2) the attorney did not promptly notify the opposing side of receipt; (3) to the extent the attorney reviews and digests the privileged information; (4) the significance of the privileged information; (5) the movant's fault in the disclosure; and (6) the prejudice nonmovant will suffer. Here, Mowbray asserted he did not review the draft affidavit and nothing suggests otherwise. Mowbray's actions indicate he was not trying to deceive Petitioners (D). Affirmed.

ANALYSIS

Attorneys' ethical rules contemplate mistakes. Should one attorney receive an accidental disclosure, he is not

Continued on next page.

supposed to examine the evidence, should notify opposing counsel, and return the disclosed evidence. The rules only work when everyone abides by them. If an attorney uses disclosed evidence in a case in violation of the rules, he faces disciplinary action, sanctions in the court case, disqualification, and his client could suffer litigation consequences such as dismissal.

■━━■

Confidentiality Exceptions: Physical and Financial Injury

Quick Reference Rules of Law

Hawkins v. King County

Mentally ill client (P) v. State county government (D)

Wash. Ct. App., 602 P.2d 361 (1979).

NATURE OF CASE: Appeal from dismissal of one party defendant.

FACT SUMMARY: Attorney Richard Sanders (D) represented Michael Hawkins (P) as a court-appointed defense counsel, and at his client's request, sought his client's release on bail. Sanders (D) learned of Hawkins's (P) mental illness and potential dangerousness but made no mention of either at the bail hearing. Hawkins (P) later assaulted his mother and attempted suicide resulting in the amputation of both legs. Hawkins (P) sued Sanders (D) for malpractice in failing to raise his mental illness as an issue at the bail hearing.

🏛 RULE OF LAW
The common-law duty to disclose client information during a release hearing is limited to situations where counsel is convinced the client intends to commit a crime or inflict injury upon a third party.

FACTS: Michael Hawkins (P) was arrested for marijuana possession during the time period his mother, Frances Hawkins (P), had hired counsel to assist in having her son committed. The court appointed Attorney Richard Sanders (D) to represent Michael (P) in his criminal case. Michael (P) requested release on bail and Sanders (D) agreed to seek his freedom. Frances's (P) attorney informed Sanders (D) in person and in writing of Michael's (P) mental illness and potential for dangerousness. A psychiatrist also informed Sanders (D) of Michael's (P) mental illness and potential to be a danger to himself and to others. The attorney and the psychiatrist recommended Michael (P) to remain in the state's custody for his and others' safety. Despite these recommendations, Sanders (D) requested Michael's (P) release at the bail hearing and the judge granted it. A few days later, Michael (P) assaulted Frances (P) and attempted suicide by jumping off a bridge, resulting in the amputation of both his legs. Michael (P), through his next friend Frances (P), sued King County (D), multiple other defendants, and Sanders (D). Sanders (D) moved to dismiss based on failure to state a claim and the judge granted the motion. The Hawkinses (P) appealed.

ISSUE: Is the common-law duty to disclose client information during a release hearing limited to situations where counsel is convinced the client intends to commit a crime or inflict injury upon a third party?

HOLDING AND DECISION: (Swanson, A.C.J.) Yes. The common-law duty to disclose client information during a release hearing is limited to situations where counsel is convinced the client intends to commit a crime or inflict injury upon a third party. First, the Hawkinses (P) argue Sanders (D) had a duty to disclose Michael's (P) mental state at the bail hearing or face liability for malpractice. No such duty exists because Michael (P) expressly requested release on bail, and disclosure at a bail hearing that would be detrimental to that request is not mandated by law or ethics. Second, the Hawkinses (P) argue Sanders (D) owed a duty to warn that Michael (P) was a danger to himself or others pursuant to *Tarasoff v. Regents of Univ. of Cal.*, 551 P.2d 334 (Cal. 1976). The facts in *Tarasoff* differ from this case. In *Tarasoff*, the psychiatrist knew of an imminent threat to a specific individual but did nothing to warn the individual about the threat when his patient was released from confinement. Here, Sanders (D) knew only that Michael (P) was mentally ill and might be a danger to himself or others. No specific threat was identified and no particular victim was named. He had no duty to warn Frances (P) of a threat of which she was already aware. Sanders (D) violated no duty to the Hawkinses (P) under *Tarasoff*. Affirmed.

▶ ANALYSIS

The attorney-client privilege is the client's and the attorney generally cannot violate that privilege absent express waiver by the client. The client's intention to commit a crime or harm to a third party may constitute such an express waiver. An attorney has to balance his duty to his client with his overall moral duty to public safety and the public good. When a client identifies a third party whom he intends to harm, the client has violated the attorney-client trust relationship and the attorney is free to share that confidence with proper authorities. The attorney must, however, strive to communicate only the absolute minimum necessary to protect an unwarned person.

■—■

Quicknotes

ATTORNEY-CLIENT PRIVILEGE A doctrine precluding the admission into evidence of confidential communications between an attorney and his client made in the course of obtaining professional assistance.

ATTORNEY-CLIENT RELATIONSHIP The confidential relationship established when a lawyer enters into employment with a client.

MALPRACTICE A failure to perform one's professional duties during the course of a client relationship, either intentionally or negligently or the poor or improper discharge of one's professional obligations.

■—■

Spaulding v. Zimmerman

Injured minor (P) v. Tortfeasor (D)

Minn. Sup. Ct., 116 N.W.2d 704 (1962).

NATURE OF CASE: Appeal from an order vacating a prior order approving a settlement for personal injuries.

FACT SUMMARY: In agreeing to a settlement for injuries sustained in an automobile accident, Spaulding's (P) attorneys did not know he had an aorta aneurysm possibly resulting from the accident; and Zimmerman's (D) attorneys, who did know, did not disclose it to Spaulding (P) or to the court.

🏛 RULE OF LAW

While no rule or duty requires defendants to disclose adverse knowledge when the parties are in an adversary position, once they reach an agreement to settle, defendants who fail to disclose run the risk that failure to affirmatively disclose information may form the basis for vacating a settlement.

FACTS: After Spaulding (P), a minor, was severely injured while riding in a car driven by Zimmerman (D), his father brought suit on Spaulding's (P) behalf. While Spaulding's (P) physicians did not discover that he had a life-threatening aorta aneurysm possibly resulting from the accident, a neurologist who examined Spaulding (P) for Zimmerman (D) pointed it out in his report to Zimmerman's (D) attorneys. The parties reached a settlement agreement and submitted it to the court for approval. The aorta aneurysm was never disclosed to the court. When Spaulding (P) had a subsequent checkup, his physician discovered the aneurysm. Spaulding (P) immediately had surgery. No longer a minor, Spaulding (P) brought this action for additional damages. The court vacated the prior settlement order. Zimmerman (D) appealed.

ISSUE: While no rule or duty requires defendants to disclose adverse knowledge when the parties are in an adversary position, once they reach an agreement to settle, do defendants who fail to disclose run the risk that failure to affirmatively disclose information may form the basis for vacating a settlement?

HOLDING AND DECISION: (Gallagher, J.) Yes. While no rule or duty requires defendants to disclose adverse knowledge when the parties are in an adversary position, once they reach an agreement to settle, defendants who fail to disclose run the risk that failure to affirmatively disclose information may form the basis for vacating a settlement. In vacating the settlement, the lower court found the aneurysm causally related to the accident. A settlement made on behalf of a minor may be vacated where it is shown that in the accident the minor sustained separate and distinct injuries which were not known or considered by the court at the time the settlement was approved. Here, Zimmerman's (D) counsel knew the seriousness of Spaulding's (P) disability but did not disclose it to the court. Therefore, the court did not abuse its discretion in setting aside the prior settlement. Affirmed.

▶ ANALYSIS

No canon of ethics or legal obligation required Zimmerman's (D) attorney to inform Spaulding (P) about the aneurysm or to advise the court about it. In fact, Spaulding's (P) counsel could have obtained the information through use of the available rules of discovery. Had Spaulding (P) not been a minor at the time of the settlement, the lower court declared it would have been justified in denying his motion to vacate, leaving him to whatever remedy he may have had against his doctor and his lawyer. Note, however, that the rule changes in ex parte proceedings, where a lawyer must inform the tribunal of all material facts (ABA Mode Rule 3.3).

Quicknotes

ABUSE OF DISCRETION A determination by an appellate court that a lower court's decision was based on an error of law.

DISCOVERY Pretrial procedure during which one party makes certain information available to the other.

Purcell v. District Attorney for the Suffolk District

Legal aid attorney (P) v. District attorney (D)

Mass. Sup. Jud. Ct., 676 N.E.2d 436 (1997).

NATURE OF CASE: Appeal from denial of motion to quash anticipated subpoena.

FACT SUMMARY: Jeffrey W. Purcell (P) believed his client intended to set fire to his apartment building after being evicted, so he informed authorities about that threat. At the client's trial for arson charges, the district attorney (D) subpoenaed Purcell (P) to testify about his conversation with the client. Purcell (P) successfully quashed that subpoena and the jury could not come to a verdict. On retrial, Purcell (P) moved to quash the anticipated subpoena.

RULE OF LAW

Attorney-client privilege applies to client communications made to facilitate the rendering of legal services but not to those made to facilitate legal advice in furtherance of a crime or fraud.

FACTS: Joseph Tyree received an eviction notice for his Boston apartment. He consulted Attorney Jeffrey W. Purcell (P) with Greater Boston Legal Services for advice on how to proceed. Purcell (P) decided to alert authorities after meeting with Tyree because he believed Tyree intended to set fire to the apartment building. The next day, authorities arrived to evict Tyree and discovered arson equipment, smoke detectors disabled, and gasoline poured in the building hallway. Tyree was arrested and charged with attempted arson. At trial, the district attorney (D) subpoenaed Purcell (P) to testify regarding his conversation with Tyree. Purcell (P) successfully moved to quash the subpoena. The jury subsequently failed to reach a verdict and the court declared a mistrial. The Commonwealth determined to re-try Tyree and again sought Purcell's (P) testimony. Purcell (P) moved to quash the anticipated subpoena based again on attorney-client privilege. The trial court denied the motion and ordered Purcell (P) to testify. Purcell (P) appealed.

ISSUE: Does the attorney-client privilege apply to client communications made to facilitate the rendering of legal services but not to those made to facilitate legal advice in furtherance of a crime or fraud?

HOLDING AND DECISION: (Wilkins, C.J.) Yes. Attorney-client privilege applies to client communications made to facilitate the rendering of legal services but not to those made to facilitate legal advice in furtherance of a crime or fraud. The bar commission agreed that Purcell (P) was permitted to inform authorities of his client's intent to commit a crime and/or harm to third parties. This disclosure may not be admissible in court, however. The district attorney (D) argues the crime-fraud exception

applies to the communication because Tyree may have consulted Purcell (P) to aid him in committing a crime. The district attorney (D) has the burden to prove by a preponderance of the evidence that an in camera review may result in proof that the exception applies. The judge, however, has the discretion to conduct such a review. The evidence here does not support a request the judge conduct the in camera review. The district attorney (D) did not prove by a preponderance of the evidence that Tyree consulted Purcell (P) for the purpose of obtaining advice or aid in committing a crime. The denial of the motion to quash cannot stand. Courts must be cautious in permitting the use of disclosures made only to protect others from a threat. Finally, the party asserting attorney-client privilege has the burden of proving the applicability of the privilege. The privilege applies if the client's communication was made to facilitate the rendering of legal services. The privilege would not apply if Tyree sought Purcell's (P) advice in furtherance of the attempted arson. The attorney-client privilege applies unless the crime-fraud exception applies here. Purcell (P) must demonstrate the applicability of the privilege. Vacated and remanded.

▶ ANALYSIS

The attorney-client privilege belongs to the client. If a client violates the attorney-client trust relationship by confiding an intention to harm a third party, the attorney must balance his duty to his client with his overall duty to the public safety. If an attorney shares a confidential client communication with the appropriate authorities to prevent impending harm, that attorney's duty is fulfilled. A client cannot expect the confidentiality to remain in that one instance. The information, however, does not then become treated as "general knowledge" with no remaining protections whatsoever. The confidence is used to take precautionary measures and then becomes a confidence once again.

■═■

Quicknotes

ATTORNEY-CLIENT PRIVILEGE A doctrine precluding the admission into evidence of confidential communications between an attorney and his client made in the course of obtaining professional assistance.

PREPONDERANCE OF THE EVIDENCE A standard of proof requiring the trier of fact to determine whether the fact sought to be established is more probable than not.

Continued on next page.

QUASH To vacate, annul, void.

SUBPOENA A command issued by court to compel a witness to appear at trial.

In re American Continental Corporation/Lincoln Savings & Loan Securities Litigation

Government (P) v. Bond sellers (D)

794 F. Supp. 1424 (D. Ariz. 1992).

NATURE OF CASE: Motion for summary judgment by law firm on opinion letter issue.

FACT SUMMARY: After Lincoln Savings and Loan (Lincoln) (D) failed, five separate actions were filed, with the law firm of Jones, Day, Reavis & Pogue (D) named as a defendant in four of them due to its activities on behalf of American Continental Corporation (D) and Lincoln (D).

🏛 RULE OF LAW
Reckless conduct is the highly unreasonable omission involving an extreme departure from the standards of ordinary care, which presents a danger of misleading buyers or sellers that is either known to the defendant or so obvious that the actor must have been aware of it.

FACTS: American Continental Corporation (ACC) (D) retained Jones, Day, Reavis & Pogue (Jones Day) (D) to perform a major internal audit of Lincoln Savings and Loan's (Lincoln's) (D) Federal Home Loan Bank Bond (FHLBB) compliance and to help Lincoln (D) deal with the FHLBB's direct investment regulations. Jones Day (D) found multiple regulatory violations. After Lincoln (D) failed, five separate actions were filed, with Jones Day (D) named as a defendant in four of them. Evidence showed that Jones Day (D) instructed ACC (D) in how to rectify deficiencies so that they would not be apparent to FHLBB examiners and that its attorneys participated in creating corporate resolutions to ratify forged and backdated corporate records. The firm also provided an opinion letter in an ACC (D) bond registration statement. Jones Day (D) moved for summary judgment.

ISSUE: Is reckless conduct the highly unreasonable omission involving an extreme departure from the standards of ordinary care, which presents a danger of misleading buyers or sellers that is either known to the defendant or so obvious that the actor must have been aware of it?

HOLDING AND DECISION: (Bilby, J.) Yes. Reckless conduct is the highly unreasonable omission involving an extreme departure from the standards of ordinary care, which presents a danger of misleading buyers or sellers that is either known to the defendant or so obvious that the actor must have been aware of it. The record raises material questions concerning § 10(b), Racketeer Influenced and Corrupt Organizations Act (RICO), Arizona Racketeering Act, common law fraud and deceit, and violations of Cal. Corp. Code §§ 25401 and 25504.1. A question of fact also remains as to whether buyers were injured by the Jones Day (D) opinion letter. Further, Jones Day (D) is an expert under § 11 of the Securities Act, and its advice influenced ACC/Lincoln's (D) conduct. Thus, the order denying summary judgment is affirmed.

▶ ANALYSIS
Attorneys must inform a client in a clear and direct manner when its conduct violates the law. If the conduct continues, the lawyer must withdraw if the representation will result in violation of the rules of professional conduct or other law. Jones Day (D) eventually paid a total of $75 million to settle both the claims of ACC (D) bondholders and stockholders, and the government claims against the firm.

Quicknotes

DECEIT A false statement made ether knowingly or with reckless disregard as to its truth and which is intended to induce the plaintiff to act in reliance thereon to his detriment.

FRAUD A false representation of facts with the intent that another will rely on the misrepresentation to his detriment.

RICO Racketeer Influenced and Corrupt Organization laws; federal and state statutes enacted for the purpose of prosecuting organized crime.

SUMMARY JUDGMENT Judgment rendered by a court in response to a motion by one of the parties, claiming that the lack of a question of material fact in respect to an issue warrants disposition of the issue without consideration by the jury.

Thomas H. Lee Equity Fund V, L.P. v. Mayer Brown, Rowe & Maw LLP

Investors (P) v. Brokerage law firm (D)

612 F. Supp. 2d 267, 609 F. Supp. 2d 304 (S.D.N.Y. 2009).

NATURE OF CASE: Class action seeking damages against law firm for aiding and abetting client's securities law violations.

FACT SUMMARY: Law firm aided client in securities fraud by helping to conceal fraudulent transactions.

🏛 RULE OF LAW
Under federal law, if a client commits securities fraud, a law firm is not liable for aiding the client in committing that fraud.

FACTS: Refco, Inc. was among the world's largest providers of brokerage and clearing services in the international derivatives, currency, and futures markets. Refco's business model involved extending credit to its customers so they could make larger trades. Over time, Refco began making loans without adequately assessing customers' credit-worthiness. In the late 1990s, due to several global financial crises, customers suffered huge trading losses and were unable to repay the loans. Instead of disclosing these multi-hundred million dollar losses, Refco hid the losses by essentially making loans to itself through third parties, which would remove the losses from Refco's books at the end of each fiscal period until they were returned just days after the financial period closed. These were referred to as "round-trip loans." Mayer Brown, Rowe & Maw LLP (Mayer Brown) (D) was Refco's outside counsel from 1994 to Refco's collapse in 2005. Mayer Brown (D) was familiar with Refco's operations and finances and participated in 17 rounds of the round-trip loan transactions from 2000 to 2005. Specifically, Mayer Brown (D) explained the structure and terms of the round-trip loans to potential third-party participants, negotiated the loans, and drafted and revised the documentation for the transactions. Mayer Brown (D) later concealed these losses in documents drafted for the Securities and Exchange Commission and for Refco's initial public offering, during which Refco sold approximately one-fifth of its shares to investors. In 2003, Thomas H. Lee Equity Fund V, L.P. (THL) (P) became interested in purchasing an interest in Refco. Mayer Brown (D) was responsible for responding to THL's (P) due diligence requests in connection with the purchase. In doing so, Mayer Brown (D) deliberately concealed the round-trip loans from the fund. In 2004, the fund acquired a majority ownership interest in Refco. In 2005, Refco's losses became public, its stocks plummeted, and it filed for bankruptcy. The fund suffered millions of dollars in losses as a result. Plaintiff investors brought a class action against Mayer Brown (D), claiming damages

for Mayer Brown's (D) knowledge and aid regarding Refco's fraudulent actions. THL (P) sued as well, claiming damages under common law fraud for fraudulent statements that Mayer Brown (D) made directly to THL (P). Mayer Brown (D) moved to dismiss all claims under Fed. R. Civ. P. 12(b)(6).

ISSUE: Under federal law, if a client commits securities fraud, is a law firm liable for aiding the client in committing that fraud?

HOLDING AND DECISION: (Lynch J.) No. Under federal law, if a client commits securities fraud, a law firm is not liable for aiding the client in committing that fraud. However, that firm may still be liable under state law covering common law fraud. While the complaint alleged facts that, if true, would make Mayer Brown (D) guilty of aiding and abetting the securities fraud that harmed the plaintiffs, under federal law, there is no private right of action for victims of securities fraud against those who merely—if otherwise substantially and culpably—aid a fraud that is executed by others. Section 10(b) of the Securities Exchange Act of 1934 imposes liability only on a person who makes a false or misleading statement of his own to the plaintiff. Specifically, because § 10(b) only imposes liability for reliance upon a misrepresentation, the misrepresentation had to be directly attributable to the defendant. Anything short of that conduct was merely aiding and abetting, no matter how substantial that aid might be. This requirement draws a "bright line" between the conduct of a secondary actor and that of a primary violator. Ultimately, the plaintiffs were relying on statements made by Refco and passed along or repeated by Mayer Brown (D), not statements made by Mayer Brown (D) itself. Motion to dismiss denied in part and granted in part.

▶ ANALYSIS

While other professional ethics cases and criminal law in general focuses on a defendant's intent, this case largely ignored the issue of intent in favor of a bright-line rule separating secondary actors from the primary violator of the Securities Exchange Act. Other courts, most notably in *In re Enron*, 235 F. Supp. 2d 549 (S.D. Tex. 2002), have found a firm liable as a primary violator when it was consciously and deeply involved in the securities fraud undertaken by its client.

■=■

Continued on next page.

Quicknotes

BRIGHT-LINE RULE A legal rule of decision to help resolve ambiguous issues simply and in a straight-forward manner, sometimes sacrificing equity for certainty.

■═■

In re Refco Securities Litigation

Investors (P) v. Collapsed corporation (D)

2010 U.S. Dist. LEXIS 107695 (S.D.N.Y. 2010).

NATURE OF CASE: Civil RICO action.

FACT SUMMARY: Collins (D), a partner in Mayer Brown (D), conspired with Refco (D) insiders to defraud investors of millions of dollars. He was convicted for his fraudulent activities and plaintiff investors (P) sought to file RICO claims against the defendants.

🏛 RULE OF LAW
A lawyer participating in or facilitating a client's fraudulent business schemes may be criminally or civilly liable for the damages to third parties.

FACTS: Plaintiff investors (P) invested more than $450 million in Refco (D) and lost more than $245 million when Refco (D) collapsed one year later. Plaintiffs (P) alleged defendant Mayer, Brown, Rowe & Maw LLP (Mayer Brown) (D) conspired with Refco (D) insiders to defraud Plaintiffs (P) in violation of § 1962(d) of the Racketeer Influenced and Corrupt Organizations Act (RICO). Collins (D), a former Mayer Brown (D) partner, was convicted by a jury for participation in the Refco (D) fraud. Collins (D) was sentenced to seven years' imprisonment. Plaintiffs (P) filed civil RICO claims against Mayer Brown (D) and Collins (D). A Special Master was appointed and heard Mayer Brown's (D) motion to dismiss and Collins's (D) motion to dismiss. The Special Master recommended granting Mayer Brown's (D) motion and denying Collins's (D).

ISSUE: May a lawyer participating in or facilitating a client's fraudulent business schemes be criminally or civilly liable for the damages to third parties?

HOLDING AND DECISION: (Rakoff, U.S.D.J.) Yes. A lawyer participating in or facilitating a client's fraudulent business schemes may be criminally or civilly liable for the damages to third parties. A civil RICO claim may only be premised on conduct actionable as securities fraud if the defendant is criminally convicted in connection with the fraud. Plaintiffs (P) argued the "criminal conviction exception" of RICO applies to Collins (D) and Mayer Brown (D). The Government, however, did not bring charges against Mayer Brown (D) and the statute requires a person-specific conviction. Collins's (D) conviction is final for all collateral purposes, so that objection is overruled. Collins (D) also argued Plaintiffs (P) failed to sufficiently plead scienter and continuity. Plaintiffs (P) alleged Collins (D) was involved in the fraud from the beginning, directed other participants, and manufactured false documents. Those allegations are sufficient to support required scienter. Continuity is supported by Plaintiffs' (P) allegations of Collins's (D) ongoing involvement from 2000–2005 in multiple facets of the fraud. The case has settled, but the court would have granted Mayer Brown's (D) motion to dismiss with prejudice and denied Collins's (D) motion to dismiss the RICO claims.

▶ ANALYSIS

Lawyers may become more than objective outsiders when serving as long-time business advisors to clients. A lawyer must always maintain professional objectivity and distance from clients and be vigilant about ethical boundaries. Advocating for one's client does not include participation in fraudulent, harmful, or dishonest misconduct.

■■■

Quicknotes

RACKETEER INFLUENCED AND CORRUPT ORGANIZATION (RICO) Federal and state statutes enacted for the purpose of prosecuting organized crime.

SCIENTER Knowledge of certain facts; often refers to "guilty knowledge," which implicates liability.

■■■

United States v. Chen

Federal government (P) v. Importer (D)

99 F.3d 1495 (9th Cir. 1996), *cert. denied*, 520 U.S. 1167 (1997).

NATURE OF CASE: Appeal from denial of motions to quash subpoenas.

FACT SUMMARY: Chen (D), importer of goods from Asia, was allegedly engaged in tax fraud through his corporation Sunrider Corporation and TF Chen Products, Inc. The Federal Government (P) sought to prosecute Chen (D) using information and affidavits from Chen's (D) sister and former Sunrider comptroller. The Government (P) also sought the testimony of Chen's (D) attorneys based on the crime-fraud exception to the attorney-client privilege.

RULE OF LAW

The crime-fraud exception applies to the attorney-client privilege even where the attorney is innocent of wrongdoing or guilty knowledge.

FACTS: Chen (D) owns Sunrider Corporation and operates TF Chen Products, Inc., a Sunrider subsidiary. Sunrider imported goods from Asia and paid tariffs on the actual cost of the goods. Sunrider's comptroller, Jau Hwa (Chen's (D) sister), then prepared false invoices on a Hong Kong affiliate's letterhead showing the goods costing much more than they actually did. Sunrider paid income tax on the profit, which was the difference between the sale price of the goods and the fake costs. Chen (D) became concerned that the Internal Revenue Service (IRS) and U.S. Customs would communicate and learn about the difference in the cost of the goods shown on the tariff invoices versus the fake invoices. Customs permits importers to disclose underpaid tariffs before Customs independently learns of the underpayments without penalty or interest. Chen (D) consulted with his attorneys and was advised to file a Customs disclosure. This disclosure was actually a fraud because Sunrider was not underpaying the tariffs but not paying appropriate income tax. The attorneys were not aware of the alleged income tax evasion scheme. Jau Hwa left Sunrider and took several incriminating documents to the Government (P). She also informed the authorities about the alleged tax evasion scheme. The Government (P) indicted Chen (D) for conspiracy, tax evasion, and other crimes. The Government (P) subpoenaed Chen's (D) attorneys to testify about the disclosure statement and their knowledge of the fraudulent scheme, but the attorneys moved to quash based on attorney-client privilege. The trial judge denied the motion based on the crime-fraud exception to the attorney-client privilege so long as the testimony was limited even though the judge did not find evidence the attorneys knew of the alleged scheme. The attorneys appealed.

ISSUE: Does the crime-fraud exception apply to the attorney-client privilege where the attorney is innocent of wrongdoing or guilty knowledge?

HOLDING AND DECISION: (Kleinfeld, J.) Yes. The crime-fraud exception applies to the attorney-client privilege even where the attorney is innocent of wrongdoing or guilty knowledge. Clients will be frightened to tell their attorneys about the entirety of their actions if the attorneys can be forced to become government informants. The attorney-client privilege is crucial to full representation. That privilege cannot, however, shield clients from ongoing or future criminal conduct. The Government (P) here argues the privilege does not apply when the attorneys are acting as "spokespersons" for a company, Sunrider, rather than legal advisors. The attorneys here were not spokespersons such as public relations persons but were lawyers communicating their clients' desires to the court and other authorities. Not all communications are privileged, such as when the attorney does not provide legal advice, but the rebuttable presumption exists when the attorney is retained to give legal advice. Here, Chen (D) retained the attorneys to provide advice about the Customs disclosure. Further, contrary to the Government's (P) argument, Hwa had no authority to waive the attorney-client privilege held by Sunrider because she was an ex-employee and was not given authority by any current officers or management. The Government (P) then has to demonstrate the crime-fraud exception applies without Hwa's information or affidavit. The Government (P) must show a factual basis to support a good-faith belief that an in camera review of the evidence will show that the crime-fraud exception applies. Then the judge may accept in camera review. The Government (P) skipped these steps and submitted Hwa's evidence to the judge. Even absent Hwa's evidence, though, the Government (P) can make out a prima facie case that the crime-fraud exception applies. The facts outside of Hwa's disclosure of confidential information would lead a reasonable person to believe Chen (D) may have sought legal counsel for the furtherance of a crime. The attorneys here were innocent of the tax evasion scheme and had no knowledge of wrongdoing, but the client knew and the attorney-client privilege is the client's. The client waived the privilege. Affirmed.

ANALYSIS

The attorney-client privilege belongs to the client to affirm or waive. When a client engages in wrongful or deceitful

Continued on next page.

conduct, he has implicitly waived that trust relationship with the attorney. Just as when a client threatens harm to a third party, a deceitful client has waived his right to confidentiality any longer. The attorney may not have an affirmative duty to inform authorities as in the threat of a harm situation, but the attorneys cannot withhold the criminal information based on the privilege when confronted with the client's wrongdoing.

■━━■

Quicknotes

AFFIDAVIT A declaration of facts written and affirmed before a witness.

ATTORNEY-CLIENT PRIVILEGE A doctrine precluding the admission into evidence of confidential communications between an attorney and his client made in the course of obtaining professional assistance.

PRIMA FACIE CASE An action where the plaintiff introduces sufficient evidence to submit the issue to the judge or jury for determination.

QUASH To vacate, annul, void.

SUBPOENA A command issued by court to compel a witness to appear at trial.

■━━■

Confidentiality Exceptions: Lawyer Interests and Compliance with Other Law

Quick Reference Rules of Law

Meyerhofer v. Empire Fire & Marine Insurance Co.

Investor (P) v. Corporation (D)

497 F.2d 1190 (2d Cir.), *cert. denied*, 419 U.S. 998 (1974).

NATURE OF CASE: Appeal from the dismissal of a class action for violation of the Securities Exchange Act and common law negligence, fraud, and deceit.

FACT SUMMARY: After Attorney Goldberg (D) was charged with making materially false and misleading statements in connection with a registration statement related to a public offering by Empire Fire and Marine Insurance Company (Empire) (D), he gave investor Meyerhofer's (P) counsel a copy of an affidavit containing confidential information received from Goldberg's (D) former client, Empire (D).

RULE OF LAW
A lawyer may reveal confidences or secrets necessary to defend himself against an accusation of wrongful conduct.

FACTS: In making a public offering of stock, Empire Fire and Marine Insurance Company (Empire) (D) was represented by Sitomer, Sitomer & Porges (Sitomer) (D). Goldberg (D) was an attorney in the firm and had done some work on the issue. Meyerhofer (P) and Federman (P), who were purchasers of Empire (D) stock, sustained losses when the market price of the stock dropped. They brought a class action suit against Empire (D), alleging, among other things, failure to disclose a large finder's fee arrangement with Sitomer (D). Bernson, Hoeniger, Freitag & Abbey represented Meyerhofer (P) and Federman (P). Goldberg (D) gave Bernson a copy of an affidavit to verify his non-participation in the finder's fee omission. The district court ordered that the Bernson firm and Goldberg (D) be barred from acting as counsel for Meyerhofer (P) in this or any future action against Empire (D) involving the transactions at issue here and then dismissed Meyerhofer's (P) complaint without prejudice. All parties appealed.

ISSUE: May, a lawyer reveal confidences or secrets necessary to defend himself against an accusation of wrongful conduct?

HOLDING AND DECISION: (Moore, J.) Yes. A lawyer may reveal confidences or secrets necessary to defend himself against an accusation of wrongful conduct. In this case, the charge of knowing participation in the filing of a false and misleading registration statement was a serious one. Thus, Goldberg (D) had the right to make an appropriate disclosure about his role in the public offering and to support his version of the facts with suitable evidence. Nevertheless, an attorney may not represent a party in a suit against a former client where there may be the appearance of a possible violation of confidence. Accord-

ingly, the district court's order prohibiting Goldberg (D) from representing the interests of Meyerhofer (P) and enjoining him from disclosing material information except on discovery or at trial is affirmed. However, since the Bernson firm's relationship with Goldberg (D) was not tainted by violations of the Code of Professional Responsibility, the order dismissing the action and enjoining Bernson from acting as counsel is reversed.

▶ ANALYSIS

The Model Rule applied here is 1.6(b)(5) and is one of the self-defense exceptions to confidentiality. Comment to Rule 1.6 reveals that the lawyer's right to respond arises when an assertion of complicity has been made. The Model Code of Professional Responsibility does not distinguish between accusations made by a third party and those made by a client.

Quicknotes

AFFIDAVIT A declaration of facts written and affirmed before a witness.

DECEIT A false statement made ether knowingly or with reckless disregard as to its truth and which is intended to induce the plaintiff to act in reliance thereon to his detriment.

DISMISSAL WITHOUT PREJUDICE A final determination of an action without a trial on the merits, allowing the parties from bringing the same action at a later date.

FRAUD A false representation of facts with the intent that another will rely on the misrepresentation to his detriment.

People v. Belge

State government (P) v. Attorney (D)

N.Y. App. Div., 372 N.Y.S.2d 798 (1975), *affirmed*, N.Y. Ct. App., 359 N.E.2d 377 (1976).

NATURE OF CASE: Motion to dismiss indictment.

FACT SUMMARY: Francis R. Belge (D) represented a criminal defendant charged with murder and put forth an insanity defense. Part of the defense included the client admitting to three other murders. Belge (D) investigated the claims, personally inspected the body of one of the victims to determine identification, and maintained the client's confidentiality until trial. At trial, the public became outraged at Belge's (D) actions and the State Government (P) received an indictment against Belge (D) for violating Public Health Laws. Belge (D) moves to dismiss the indictment.

🏛 RULE OF LAW
Attorney-client privilege may outweigh administration of justice even when the attorney is informed of information relevant to a criminal investigation but does not inform the authorities.

FACTS: Francis R. Belge (D) and Frank H. Armani represented Robert F. Garrow, Jr. in Garrow's trial for murder. Counsel advanced a defense of insanity. Garrow admitted to Belge (D) and Armani he had committed three other murders. Belge (D) drove to the alleged burial site of one of the victims, personally inspected the body, and confirmed to his own satisfaction the identity of the victim. Belge (D) did not, however, inform authorities of the location of the body or the admission of his client. At trial, Garrow testified to the murders in support of his insanity defense. The public became outraged that Belge (D) had failed to inform authorities of his client's information. The State (P) charged Belge (D) with violation of two Public Health Laws: prohibiting a decent burial of the dead and failing to report a medically unattended death to the authorities. Belge (D) moved to dismiss the indictments.

ISSUE: Does the attorney-client privilege outweigh administration of justice even when the attorney is informed of information relevant to a criminal investigation but does not inform the authorities?

HOLDING AND DECISION: (Gale, J.) Yes. Attorney-client privilege may outweigh administration of justice even when the attorney is informed of information relevant to a criminal investigation but does not inform the authorities. Here, the public hue and cry was against Belge's (D) apparent obstruction of justice in preventing authorities from solving the murder of another of Garrow's victims. The public believed Belge (D) should have weighed his client's confidentiality against public decency and general morality. Garrow, however, is constitutionally entitled to protection against self-incrimination. That constitutional right would be violated if the attorney in whom Garrow confided passed on the confidence to authorities. The court would have a more difficult problem if Belge (D) had been indicted for obstruction of justice, but the violations of the Public Health Laws clearly fall when compared to the sanctity of attorney-client privilege and protection of a criminal defendant's constitutional rights. The indictment is dismissed.

▶ ANALYSIS

Criminal attorneys arguably have a tougher balancing act than other attorneys when it comes to client confidentiality versus moral duty to the public. Garrow was not threatening imminent harm to an unknowing third party, so the attorneys had no obligation to notify authorities of a potential crime. Garrow was not using his attorneys in furtherance of an ongoing or future criminal act, so the attorneys did not have to worry about a crime-fraud exception to the confidentiality. The attorneys here did have to weigh their client's constitutional rights against public decency in letting a family know of a lost daughter's location. They may not have made a morally popular decision, but they made a proper legal decision.

Quicknotes

ATTORNEY-CLIENT PRIVILEGE A doctrine precluding the admission into evidence of confidential communications between an attorney and his client made in the course of obtaining professional assistance.

MOTION TO DISMISS Motion to terminate an action based on the adequacy of the pleadings, improper service or venue, etc.

People v. Casey

State government (P) v. Attorney (D)

Colo. Sup. Ct., 948 P.2d 1014 (1997).

NATURE OF CASE: Appeal from imposition of disciplinary sanctions.

FACT SUMMARY: Attorney Casey (D) represented a teenager who had used a friend's identity in criminal trespass proceedings. Casey (D) did not inform the court of his client's true identity, resulting in an unjustified criminal history for the friend. Casey (D) admitted to violations of the disciplinary code but believed the recommended sanctions were too harsh.

🏛 RULE OF LAW
The attorney-client privilege does not override the attorney's duty to be truthful to the court even where that would result in disclosure of otherwise confidential communications.

FACTS: S.R., a teenager, was at a party when authorities arrived and arrested partygoers with criminal trespass. S.R. gave authorities the driver's license of a friend, S.J., and maintained her identity was S.J. A hearing was set with S.J. as the defendant, but S.J. was unaware of the charges against her and S.R. did not inform her. Neither S.J. nor S.R. attended the hearing and a bench warrant was issued in S.J.'s name. S.R. later appeared to have the hearing re-set and continued the deception about her identity as S.J. A few months later, S.R. and her mother met with a senior partner at Casey's (D) firm. The partner assigned the case to Casey (D) who represented S.R. in her criminal trespass proceedings. Casey (D) informed the City Attorney that he represented S.J., he conducted discovery in S.J.'s name, and entered an appearance "on behalf of S.J.," despite the fact he never represented S.J. and only represented S.R. Casey (D) did not inform the City Attorney or the Court about S.R.'s true identity. Casey (D) negotiated the dismissal of the charges against S.J. and informed S.J. and her stepfather they would have to petition the court to seal her criminal record. S.J. was angry that she had a criminal record at all when S.R. was the true criminal defendant, so she and her stepfather consulted another attorney. That attorney notified the district attorney. Casey (D) stipulated he had violated multiple disciplinary codes but claimed the defense of attorney-client privilege as to his client's true identity. The hearing panel and hearing board recommended a 45-day suspension and requirement that Casey (D) take and pass the Multi-State Professional Responsibility Examination. Casey (D) appealed on the basis the sanctions are too severe.

ISSUE: Does the attorney-client privilege override the attorney's duty to be truthful to the court where that would result in disclosure of otherwise confidential communications?

HOLDING AND DECISION: (Per curiam) No. The attorney-client privilege does not override the attorney's duty to be truthful to the court even where that would result in disclosure of otherwise confidential communications. Casey (D) had a duty to inform the court of S.R.'s true identity and her past actions of pretending to be S.J. Casey (D) also appears to claim protection as a subordinate acting pursuant to a supervisory attorney's direction. The senior partner admittedly "consulted and advised" Casey (D) but no evidence exists to suggest when that occurred or to what extent. Such consultation may mitigate the severity of Casey's (D) conduct, but cannot do so here when the extent is unknown. Affirmed.

▶ ANALYSIS

It could almost be argued here that the crime-fraud exception exists to S.R.'s communications with Casey (D) because she was using the attorney in furtherance of her ongoing identity theft. Attorneys cannot become a part of an individual client's criminal schemes when the overarching duty of an attorney is to be an officer of the court.

Quicknotes

ATTORNEY-CLIENT PRIVILEGE A doctrine precluding the admission into evidence of confidential communications between an attorney and his client made in the course of obtaining professional assistance.

In re Forrest

Disciplined attorney (D)

N.J. Sup. Ct., 730 A.2d 340 (1999).

NATURE OF CASE: Disciplinary action against attorney.

FACT SUMMARY: Attorney Forrest (D) represented the Fennimores in their personal injury action. Mr. Fennimore passed away and Forrest (D) did not notify the court or opposing counsel. Forrest (D) obtained an arbitration award on Mr. Fennimore's behalf and still failed to notify the parties about his death. The Disciplinary Oversight Committee brought disciplinary action against Forrest (D) for violations of professional ethics rules in connection with his deliberate concealment of the death of his client.

🏛 RULE OF LAW
Counsel may not misrepresent a material fact to the court and opposing counsel as a tactic of zealous advocacy.

FACTS: Mr. and Mrs. Fennimore retained Forrest's (D) law firm to represent them in a personal injury suit against a driver who hit their automobile. Mr. Fennimore passed away due to causes unrelated to the accident and Mrs. Fennimore notified Forrest (D) of the death. Forrest (D) served unsigned interrogatory answers on behalf of Mr. Fennimore upon opposing counsel without notifying opposing counsel of Mr. Fennimore's death. Forrest (D) encouraged Mrs. Fennimore to say her husband was unavailable when questioned in depositions. Forrest (D) also informed an arbitrator during mandatory arbitration on the case that Mr. Fennimore was unavailable. At no time during hearings, discovery, or settlement conferences did Forrest (D) inform the court or opposing counsel about Mr. Fennimore's death. The arbitrator recommended an award to Mrs. Fennimore of $17,500 and to Mr. Fennimore of $6,000. Opposing counsel then inquired about Mr. Fennimore's availability for a medical exam. Forrest (D) did not respond. Opposing counsel filed a motion to compel Mr. Fennimore to submit to a physical exam, which the judge granted after Forrest (D) did not respond or appear at the hearing to contest the motion. When Mr. Fennimore missed his court-ordered appointment for the examination, Forrest (D) admitted to the death. The Disciplinary Oversight Committee sought to discipline Forrest (D) for failing to disclose a material fact to the tribunal, obstructing opposing counsel's access to evidence of potential evidentiary value, and engaging in dishonest conduct. Forrest (D) conceded he should have disclosed the fact of Mr. Fennimore's death and was sorry for his actions.

ISSUE: May counsel misrepresent a material fact to the court and opposing counsel as a tactic of zealous advocacy?

HOLDING AND DECISION: (Per curiam) No. Counsel may not misrepresent a material fact to the court and opposing counsel as a tactic of zealous advocacy. Forrest (D) affirmatively encouraged his client to conceal her husband's death, he failed to notify the arbitrator of the death, and he breached his duty of candor to the court and opposing counsel. Forrest (D) also misled opposing counsel when he sent unsigned interrogatory answers and attempted to negotiate a settlement on his deceased client's behalf. Forrest (D) does have an obligation to zealously advocate for his client, but not when such advocacy results in deception before the court and opposing counsel. Forrest (D) continued to engage in deceitful conduct over a period of nine months. Forrest (D) does understand the serious breach, but sanctions are important for such transgressions. Forrest (D) is suspended for six months and must reimburse the Disciplinary Oversight Committee for administrative costs.

▮ ANALYSIS

The judicial system cannot work if all of the players engage in deceit and misinformation. The whole point of protecting attorney-client confidences is to encourage truthful communications and use those communications to the best strategic advantage in arriving at the truth of any case. If the court and opposing counsel cannot rely on the representations of an attorney, the litigation system fails. Zealous advocacy on behalf of a client means advocating for that client's truth and not putting forth lies to win.

▬▬

Quicknotes

ATTORNEY-CLIENT PRIVILEGE A doctrine precluding the admission into evidence of confidential communications between an attorney and his client made in the course of obtaining professional assistance.

BREACH The violation of an obligation imposed pursuant to contract or law, by acting or failing to act.

▬▬

Matter of Hendrix

Debtor driver (D)

986 F.2d 195 (7th Cir. 1993).

NATURE OF CASE: Appeal from grant of motion to modify bankruptcy order to permit proceeding against debtor's insurer.

FACT SUMMARY: Hendrix (D) declared bankruptcy and listed the Pages as creditors who had a personal injury judgment against him. The Pages did not file a claim and Hendrix's (D) debt to the Pages was discharged. The Pages moved the bankruptcy judge to modify the bankruptcy order to permit them to proceed in state court against Hendrix's (D) liability insurer. The judge granted the motion and the insurer appealed. The insurer failed to cite a contrary dispositive case in its appeal brief.

⚖ RULE OF LAW
Failure to cite dispositive contrary authority or argue for its overruling is sanctionable conduct.

FACTS: Hendrix (D) was driving an automobile that injured Sara Page. The Pages won a personal injury judgment against Hendrix (D), who had liability insurance, but Hendrix (D) declared bankruptcy. He listed the Pages as creditors but the Pages never filed a claim. Hendrix's (D) debts, including to the Pages, were discharged. The Pages later moved the bankruptcy court to modify the bankruptcy order to permit them to proceed in state court against Hendrix's (D) liability insurer, Atlanta Casualty Company. The bankruptcy judge granted the motion and the district judge affirmed. Atlanta Casualty Company filed an appeal. One particular case was dispositive on the issue of whether the Pages could proceed against a debtor's insurer when the debt had been discharged as to the insured personally. The case supported the Pages' position. Neither the insurer's attorney nor the Pages' attorney cited the case, however.

ISSUE: Is the failure to cite dispositive contrary authority or argue for its overruling sanctionable conduct?

HOLDING AND DECISION: (Posner, J.) Yes. Failure to cite dispositive contrary authority or argue for its overruling is sanctionable conduct. The insurer's appeal could not succeed unless the insurer successfully argued for this court to overrule *Shondel*, 950 F.2d 1301 (7th Cir. 1991), which was decided long before this appeal. The insurer, however, failed to even cite *Shondel*. The omission by the insurer is disturbing because insurance companies are sophisticated enterprises in legal matters, *Shondel* was an insurance case and the law firm that handled this appeal for the insurer is located in this circuit. The Pages' attorney is a solo practitioner in a nonmetropolitan area, so it is slightly more understandable that he did not find *Shondel*

and he cannot be accused of hiding contrary authority from the court because it is directly in favor of his client's position. The insurer filed a frivolous appeal because it did not cite the controlling authority or argue for overruling it. Pursuant to Fed. R. App. P. 38 sanctions are appropriate for the frivolous appeal. A question arises whether the insurer's counsel deliberately failed to cite *Shondel*, which is professional misconduct, or only filed the appeal for purposes of delay, which is also sanctionable. Further, the attorney who signed the briefs on behalf of the insurer had a Fed. R. Civ. P. 11-duty to ensure the arguments were not frivolous, so sanctions may be appropriate against the attorney also. The insurer, its counsel, and the attorney signing the briefs have 14 days to submit statements explaining why the court should not impose sanctions.

▶ ANALYSIS

Attorneys have a duty to bring contrary authorities to the court's attention. The successful attorney then differentiates the case on the facts, legal position, or holding or argues for the overturning of that case. It is never acceptable to pretend the case does not exist or attempt to mislead the court to think that only supporting precedent is available. As the court notes, an inability to fully research an issue may somewhat excuse an oversight, but the blatant omission is not forgiven. A strong brief-writer will find supporting authority, distinguish contrary authority, and ask the court to provide relief to his client.

■=■

Quicknotes

BANKRUPTCY A legal proceeding whereby a debtor, who is unable to pay his debts as they become due, is relieved of his obligation to pay his creditors either by liquidation and distribution of his remaining assets or through reorganization and payment from future income.

SANCTIONS A penalty imposed in order to ensure compliance with a statute or regulation.

■=■

United States v. Shaffer Equipment Co.

Federal government (P) v. Waste spiller (D)

11 F.3d 450 (4th Cir. 1993).

NATURE OF CASE: Appeal from dismissal of case as sanction for attorney breach.

FACT SUMMARY: Attorneys for the United States Environmental Protection Agency (EPA) (P) deliberately concealed the misrepresented achievements and credentials of the EPA (P) On-Site Coordinator responsible for the preparation of the administrative hearing documents. The court sanctioned counsel for the concealment by dismissing the case in its entirety.

🏛 RULE OF LAW

Zealous advocacy on behalf of a client may not include misrepresenting material facts to the court or opposing counsel.

FACTS: Robert E. Caron was the On-Site Coordinator for a United States Environmental Protection Agency (EPA) (P) clean-up site. Caron claimed to have a B.S. in environmental science from Rutgers University and an M.S. in organic chemistry from Drexel, but neither university had records of Caron receiving such degrees. J. Jarod Snyder, a Department of Justice attorney, represented the EPA (P), including Caron, at depositions. Snyder was aware that Caron had not received a degree from Rutgers. Caron testified at his deposition about his alleged educational background and Snyder objected to the continued questions as irrelevant but did not reveal the truth about Caron's credentials. When defense counsel suggested obtaining a court ruling on the objection, Snyder requested a recess and contacted his superior, William A. Hutchins. Snyder was advised to inform Caron he may wish to cease answering and seek individual counsel. Caron chose to continue answering and Snyder continued to state objections to the line of questioning about Caron's credentials. Defense counsel argued the questions were relevant because they went to Caron's credibility. Snyder, after research, determined the questions were relevant but still failed to alert defense counsel or withdraw the objections. The Inspector General later opened a criminal investigation into Caron's misrepresentations, but no one alerted the court or defense counsel to the ongoing investigation. Further, Snyder based his motion for summary judgment on Caron's administrative documents although he did not cite to Caron's testimony or include Caron's affidavit. He still did not inform the court or defense counsel of Caron's misrepresented credentials. Hutchens continued to advise Snyder to delete reference to the criminal investigation in correspondence and avoid notification to the court or defense counsel. Defense counsel then independently learned Caron falsely testified in another case and so informed

the Assistant United States Attorney. At that time, EPA (P) informed the court and defense counsel of the "Caron problem" and requested a stay. The district court held that Snyder and Hutchins violated their duty of candor to the court and failed to supplement discovery with material information. The court sanctioned counsel by dismissing the action in its entirety and awarding costs to the defendant. EPA (P) appealed.

ISSUE: May zealous advocacy on behalf of a client include misrepresenting material facts to the court or opposing counsel?

HOLDING AND DECISION: (Niemeyer, J.) No. Zealous advocacy on behalf of a client may not include misrepresenting material facts to the court or opposing counsel. Attorneys, as officers of the court, must first ensure the integrity of the judicial system by advancing honesty on behalf of their clients. Here, Rule 3.3 requires candor before the tribunal and Rule 3.4 requires candor to opposing counsel. Snyder and Hutchins violated both rules as well as the general duty of candor and good faith. Rule 3.3 requires "actual knowledge" of a falsehood as well as materiality of that falsehood. EPA (P) argues its counsel had suspicions of Caron's misrepresentations, but that argument rings false when confronted with the extent and repetition of Caron's fraudulent claims. Snyder had direct knowledge that Caron did not have a degree from Rutgers, did not correct Caron's false testimony in his deposition, did not correct Caron's fraudulent employment application with the EPA (P), and relied on Caron's complied administrative record for the summary judgment motion. The EPA (P) certainly had actual knowledge of Caron's lack of credibility. Next, the court must consider whether the falsehoods were material to the case. The EPA (P) had to prove that its costs incurred in cleaning defendant's site were due to defendant's release or threatened release of hazardous waste. The costs occurred because of Caron's recommendations and the administrative record supporting the costs was compiled at Caron's direction. Thus, Caron's credibility was relevant and material to the case. In fact, Snyder discovered the relevancy in his own legal research. The final factor to consider is whether Caron's conduct is a fraudulent act of the EPA (P). It is characterized as such because Caron is an important witness for EPA's (P) case, the EPA (P) covered up his misrepresentations made during his employ with the EPA (P), and did so for the purpose of disguising a weakness in the case. The attorneys placed themselves at risk for sanction in overstepping the bounds of zealous advocacy on behalf of the

Continued on next page.

EPA (P). Dismissal, however, was too severe a sanction. The defendants would benefit to a greater degree than the harm caused by the attorney's breach. The court affirms the existence of a breach but vacates the order of dismissal and remands for imposition of a sanction short of dismissal. Affirmed in part; vacated in part; and remanded.

▌ *ANALYSIS*

The judicial system relies on the general honesty of its participants. Justice is served when the truth is uncovered and the appropriate parties receive the appropriate relief; whether that is civil relief or criminal punishment. When attorneys participate in putting forth misrepresentations, deceit, or outright lies, the judicial system fails. When an attorney uncovers a discrepancy in a client's story, background, or credentials, the attorney generally has plenty of opportunity to correct the misrepresentation, counsel the client appropriately to avoid further harm, or find a replacement witness/expert/theory. Here, the attorneys let opportunity after opportunity pass them by while they engaged in the client's deceit. This undermines the overall integrity of the system and justice cannot be served.

Quicknotes

BREACH The violation of an obligation imposed pursuant to contract or law, by acting or failing to act.

MOTION FOR SUMMARY JUDGMENT Judgment rendered by a court in response to a motion by one of the parties, claiming that the lack of a question of material fact in respect to an issue warrants disposition of the issue without consideration by the jury.

SANCTIONS A penalty imposed in order to ensure compliance with a statute or regulation.

STAY An order by a court requiring a party to refrain from a specific activity until the happening of an event or upon further action by the court.

Nguyen v. Knowles

Convicted felon (D) v. [Party unidentified in casebook] (P)

2010 U.S. Dist. Lexis 89894 (E.D. Cal.), *aff'd*, 2010 U.S. Dist. Lexis 97816 (2010).

NATURE OF CASE: Writ of habeas corpus.

FACT SUMMARY: Henry (D)'s attorney, Mr. Sullivan, believed Henry (D) would commit perjury on the defense stand. He informed the judge of that belief although he admitted he had no first-hand knowledge. The judge and Mr. Sullivan discussed Mr. Sullivan's ethical obligations off the record, in camera, out of Henry's (D) and the prosecutor's presence. Henry (D) subsequently testified in narrative form without Mr. Sullivan eliciting any testimony. He was convicted and sentenced to twenty-three years and eight months in state prison.

🏛 RULE OF LAW
An attorney must have a firm factual basis to support a belief of client misconduct before acting on that belief or involving the tribunal to address the belief.

FACTS: A group of masked men robbed a casino. Victims identified the perpetrators as Asian men, one spoke Vietnamese, and one was called "Bao." Police identified Minh as a participant and Minh led police to "Henry" Nguyen (Henry) (D). Prosecutors filed charges against Henry and the case went to a jury trial. Prior to Henry's (D) testimony at trial, Henry's (D) counsel, Mr. Salinger, spoke with the court ex parte about an ethical conflict. The court determined Henry (D) did not need to be present for further discussion and the prosecutor also was excused. On the record, the court and Mr. Salinger agreed the issue to be discussed was Mr. Salinger's belief his client intended to perjure himself on the stand. Mr. Salinger and the judge held a conference off the record and then went back on the record with the decision. The judge confirmed Mr. Salinger had advised Henry (D) of the crime of perjury, the strategic disadvantage of committing perjury, and his obligation to be truthful. Mr. Salinger believed he could continue to represent Henry (D) as long as he did not elicit the perjured testimony and Henry (D) testified in narrative form. The judge agreed with that determination. Mr. Salinger stated he did not have first-hand knowledge that Henry's (D) testimony would be perjurious, but Henry (D) told him one version of events the first time and a completely different version of events the second time. Henry (D) testified through an interpreter and testified in a narrative fashion. The jury found Henry (D) guilty and the judge sentenced him to four years longer than the probation department recommended. The judge specifically referenced Henry (D) lying to the jury when he sentenced Henry (D). [Henry (D) filed a writ of habeas corpus.]

ISSUE: Must an attorney have a firm factual basis to support a belief of client misconduct before acting on that belief or involving the tribunal to address the belief?

HOLDING AND DECISION: (Moulds, J.) Yes. An attorney must have a firm factual basis to support a belief of client misconduct before acting on that belief or involving the tribunal to address the belief. Henry (D) first claimed he had a constitutional right to be present during the conference between the judge and Mr. Sullivan because it was a critical stage of the proceedings. Henry (D) averted his testimony was truthful and Mr. Sullivan misunderstood the intended testimony because of a language barrier. Henry (D) had a due process right to be present at the meeting, but the court could conclude the resulting narrative testimony was harmful to Henry (D). The jury heard Henry's (D) testimony and chose to disbelieve him. No evidence supports a belief the jury would have found otherwise had Mr. Sullivan participated in eliciting testimony from Henry (D). The next claim was that Mr. Sullivan provided ineffective assistance of counsel. Henry (D) must first prove Mr. Sullivan's performance fell below an objective standard of reasonableness and then that he was prejudiced by that performance. Here, there is no evidence Henry (D) told Mr. Sullivan he intended to commit perjury. Mr. Sullivan should have had a "firm factual basis" to believe his client intended to commit perjury before acting on that belief. Mr. Sullivan told the judge he had no first-hand knowledge of the perjury. The decision to inform the court of suspected perjury was outside the bounds of reasonably competent professional assistance. No evidence suggests, however, Henry (D) was prejudiced by Mr. Sullivan's performance because nothing indicates the outcome of Henry's (D) trial would have been any different. The evidence does indicate the sentencing might have been different. The judge specifically referenced Henry's (D) "lying," "perjured himself," and "conduct in this case" when sentencing Henry (D) to twenty-three years and eight months in state prison. Henry (D) is not entitled to relief from his conviction, but he is entitled to relief from the sentence imposed by the trial court. The Sixth Amendment violation occurred at the in camera meeting and the prejudice occurred at the sentencing. State has thirty days to decide to retry or resentence Henry (D). Writ granted.

▶ ANALYSIS

An attorney cannot participate, support, or encourage client misconduct and zealous advocacy on behalf of a client

Continued on next page.

does not privilege otherwise prohibited behavior. An attorney cannot, however, report client misconduct without facts backing up suspicion. The attorney is otherwise putting himself at risk for ethical violations and his client at risk of prejudice before the jury or tribunal.

■━■

Quicknotes

IN CAMERA In private chambers.

PERJURY The making of false statements under oath.

WRIT OF HABEAS CORPUS A proceeding in which a defendant brings a writ to compel a judicial determination of whether he is lawfully being held in custody.

■━■

Conflicts of Interest: Loyalty and Independent Judgment

Quick Reference Rules of Law

Maritrans GP Inc. v. Pepper, Hamilton & Scheetz

Petroleum transportation company (P) v. Law firm (D)

Pa. Sup. Ct., 602 A.2d 1277 (1992).

NATURE OF CASE: Appeal from grant of preliminary injunction.

FACT SUMMARY: Pepper, Hamilton & Scheetz (Pepper) (D) represented Maritrans GP Inc. (Maritrans) (P) in its labor relations, corporate, and securities matters over a decade. Pepper (D) learned a great deal of Maritrans's (P) confidential corporate information during the representation. Pepper (D) then undertook representation of Maritrans's (P) competitors contrary to Maritrans's (P) express wishes. Maritrans (P) then fired Pepper (D) and Pepper (D) accepted representation of Maritrans's (P) biggest competitor. Maritrans (P) filed this action claiming Pepper (D) breached its duty by engaging in conflicts of interest.

🏛 RULE OF LAW
It is an impermissible conflict of interest for an attorney to represent a subsequent client whose interests are materially adverse to a former client in a matter substantially related to matters in which he represented the former client.

FACTS: Maritrans GP Inc. (Maritrans) (P) is a petroleum transportation company based in Philadelphia. Pepper, Hamilton & Scheetz (Pepper) (D), a Philadelphia law firm, represented Maritrans (P) for over a decade for its labor relations matters. Pepper (D) then began representing Maritrans (P) in its corporate and securities matters. Pepper (D) accepted approximately $2 million in fees over the years from Maritrans (P). Pepper (D), and one Pepper (D) attorney particularly, Messina, engaged in in-depth review of Maritrans (P) business practices, labor practices, and comparisons to competitors locally and those based in New York. The labor practices and costs were particularly sensitive because that is the area in which the transportation businesses truly competed with one another. Messina began representing four New York-based Maritrans (P) competitors in a union negotiation which would permit those companies to become more competitive with Maritrans (P). Maritrans (P) objected but Pepper (D) claimed the conflict was a "business conflict" rather than a "legal conflict" and was not a breach of its fiduciary duty to Maritrans (P). Maritrans (P) did not want Pepper (D) to represent its biggest New York competitor, so Maritrans (P) agreed to allow Pepper (D) to continue representation of the four if Pepper (D) would limit representation to only those four and set up an ethical wall between the attorneys representing Maritrans (P) and Messina who was representing the four. Unbeknownst to Maritrans (P), Messina "parked" the biggest competitor with another labor attorney who was negotiating to become a Pepper (D) part-

ner. Maritrans (P) soon fired Pepper (D), the labor attorney became a partner and brought in the biggest competitor, and Maritrans (P) filed a complaint. Maritrans (P) alleged Pepper (D) and Messina breached their fiduciary duties to Maritrans (P) because they engaged in conflicts of interest. The trial court granted Maritrans (P) a preliminary injunction enjoining Pepper (D) and Messina from representation of the Maritrans (P) competitors. Pepper (D) appealed.

ISSUE: Is it an impermissible conflict of interest for an attorney to represent a subsequent client whose interests are materially adverse to a former client in a matter substantially related to matters in which he represented the former client?

HOLDING AND DECISION: (Papadakos, J.) Yes. It is an impermissible conflict of interest for an attorney to represent a subsequent client whose interests are materially adverse to a former client in a matter substantially related to matters in which he represented the former client. Attorneys are bound by fiduciary duty to their clients and failure to perform gives rise to a cause of action. The client's cause of action differs from disciplinary action against the attorney for the ethical violation. Civil sanctions against the attorneys may be appropriate, including disgorgement of fees. Injunctive relief is appropriate where the threat to breach fiduciary duty exists and an injury looms that cannot be compensated for by damages. The facts here demonstrate the appropriateness of a preliminary injunction against Pepper (D) while a blanket rule that a law firm cannot represent a business competitor of a former client is unnecessary. Maritrans's (P) competitive position could be irreparably injured with little ability to determine damages because the courts would have to inquire into the confidential communications between Pepper (D) and its new clients. Affirmed.

▶ ANALYSIS

Attorneys have an obligation to act in the best interests of their client. If an attorney's personal interests would interfere with the client's interests that is by definition a conflict of interest. Here, Messina's personal interest in obtaining more clients (and ostensibly a greater salary) interfered with his obligations to act in the best interest of his longtime client. If an attorney recognizes a conflict of interest, he can seek the client's consent to that conflict in writing. If consent is not given, the attorney's duty is to his existing client and not himself.

■=■

Continued on next page.

Quicknotes

BREACH The violation of an obligation imposed pursuant to contract or law, by acting or failing to act.

BREACH OF FIDUCIARY DUTY The failure of a fiduciary to observe the standard of care exercised by professionals of similar education and experience.

CAUSE OF ACTION A fact or set of facts the occurrence of which entitles a party to seek judicial relief.

ENJOIN The ordering of a party to cease the conduct of a specific activity.

INJUNCTIVE RELIEF A court order issued as a remedy, requiring a person to do, or prohibiting that person from doing, a specific act.

PRELIMINARY INJUNCTION A judicial mandate issued to require or restrain a party from certain conduct; used to preserve a trial's subject matter or to prevent threatened injury.

Murray v. Village of Hazel Crest

Former officer (P) v. City government (D)

2006 U.S. Dist. LEXIS 89388 (N.D. Ill.).

NATURE OF CASE: Motion to disqualify counsel in discrimination case.

FACT SUMMARY: The same two attorneys represented four plaintiffs in separate but related cases. The attorneys argued the plaintiffs were willing to accept lower damages, but Village of Hazel Crest (D) argued the conflict required disqualification.

🏛 RULE OF LAW
An attorney must make full disclosure of conflicts of interest, and, if waiver of the conflict is possible, obtain a waiver from each affected client.

FACTS: Former police sergeants Patrick Murray (P), Michael Garofalo, David Nelson, and Mark Peers brought four separate, but related, cases against Village of Hazel Crest (Village) (D) alleging Village (D) improperly discriminated against the plaintiffs when it promoted a less-qualified African-American to the position of deputy chief of police. Attorneys Patricia Rummer and Richard Lowell represent each plaintiff in each of the four proceedings. Village (D) moved to disqualify Rummer and Lowell on the basis of conflict of interest. The four plaintiffs had to each prove he was the more qualified candidate to get damages. Village (D) claimed Rummer and Lowell cannot claim all four clients were the one person most qualified.

ISSUE: Must an attorney make full disclosure of conflicts of interest, and, if waiver of the conflict is possible, obtain a waiver from each affected client?

HOLDING AND DECISION: (Hart, J.) Yes. An attorney must make full disclosure of conflicts of interest, and, if waiver of the conflict is possible, obtain a waiver from each affected client. Village (D) has a defense that each plaintiff would not have been promoted even absent discrimination. The proof is that another applicant would have been selected. Thus, the plaintiff's attorney must gather and present evidence the particular plaintiff is the most qualified over any other candidate. Each plaintiff will be in competition against the other for the lost wages claims. Rummer and Lowell argue the four clients are willing to forgo larger damages awards in the interest of cost-sharing counsel. They claim the clients want them to continue representing everyone. However, there is no evidence the plaintiffs have been fully advised of the potential for conflict. The conflict may be waivable, but nothing indicates the proper and full disclosures were made to the plaintiffs. The plaintiffs do have a common interest in showing the existing deputy chief of police was promoted because of his race and there may be a real interest in cost-

sharing. The conflict, however, will have a substantial impact on the damages recovered. A disinterested attorney recommends each plaintiff should have his own attorney. Village (D) also argues Rummer and Lowell should be disqualified from representing any plaintiff. Rule 1.9 applies to the extent any one plaintiff revealed confidential information to the attorneys which could be used to the disadvantage of the other plaintiffs. Counsel must consider whether continued representation is appropriate and obtain the approval of the remaining plaintiffs after full disclosure. Granted.

▶ ANALYSIS

Attorneys can enter into joint representation agreements, but the clients must understand fully the consequences of such joint representation. A conflict of interest may be unavoidable and the clients can only waive the conflict after full and complete disclosure of the conflict and its effect on the individual client's matter.

■■■

Quicknotes

CONFLICT OF INTEREST Refers to ethical problems that arise, or may be anticipated to arise, between an attorney and his client if the interests of the attorney, another client or a third-party conflict with those of the present client.

■■■

Sanford v. Commonwealth of Virginia

Heirs of deceased (P) v. State (D)

687 F. Supp. 2d 591 (E.D. Va. 2009).

NATURE OF CASE: Motion to disqualify counsel in wrongful death action.

FACT SUMMARY: Sanford (P) was a post-operative patient at Medical College of Virginia Main Hospital (MCV) and he experienced delirium over a period of days. During one bout of delirium, MCV medical staff contacted Virginia Commonwealth University Police Department (VCUPD) officers to restrain Sanford (P) and the medical staff injected him with Haldol. Thirty minutes into the restraints, Sanford (P) died. Two attorneys represented multiple defendants in the ensuing litigation.

🏛 RULE OF LAW
An attorney owes loyalty and independent judgment to each client with an appropriate course of action for each client, and if a conflict arises after representation has begun, the attorney should withdraw.

FACTS: John Charles Sanford (P) was a patient in the Medical College of Virginia Main Hospital (MCV) recovering from an operation to remove his kidney. Sanford (P) suffered from Biemond's Syndrome, which resulted in him shaking almost continuously and required him to wear knee-to-foot leg braces. Two days after his surgery, Sanford's (P) brother found Sanford (P) outside his room naked, delirious, and trying to stand without a walker. The MCV staff, aware of Sanford's (P) condition, had summoned the Virginia Commonwealth University Police Department (VCUPD) to restrain Sanford (P). Before the VCUPD arrived, however, Sanford's (P) brother penetrated the delirium and returned him to his bed. A day later, other family members found Sanford (P) on his room's floor cleaning up imaginary blood. They determined he was not being attended by any physician or nurse and requested a psychiatric consult and liaison service. One day later, Sanford (P) again became delirious, the VCUPD arrived and cuffed Sanford's (P) hands behind his back, Sanford (P) was held facedown for thirty minutes, and a nurse injected him with Haldol. After thirty minutes, the VCUPD officers and nursing staff turned Sanford (P) over and discovered he was dead. The family alleged Sanford's (P) delirium was caused by medication given him by the MCV medical staff. One attorney represents all of the VCUPD officer defendants and the supervisor, Colonel Fuller. Another attorney represents all of the MCV medical defendants and the security guard Lancaster. Plaintiffs filed a motion to disqualify both attorneys.

ISSUE: Does an attorney owe loyalty and independent judgment to each client with an appropriate course of

action for each client, and if a conflict arises after representation has begun, should the attorney withdraw?

HOLDING AND DECISION: (Payne, J.) Yes. An attorney owes loyalty and independent judgment to each client with an appropriate course of action for each client, and if a conflict arises after representation has begun, the attorney should withdraw. Each attorney claims each met with their respective clients and obtained consent to joint representation. Plaintiffs first allege a conflict among the VCUPD defendants. Colonel Fuller and the subordinate VCUPD officers have a conflict because of the issue of training. Colonel Fuller admitted the VCUPD officers received no special training on restraining hospital patients but know to check for signs of physical distress in hand-cuffed persons. Some of the other officer defendants argue it was the lack of training, and not the individual conduct, which resulted in Sanford's (P) death. Second, some of the officers have an argument they were following orders of first-responders. That does not excuse their conduct, but it may go to the assessment of the reasonableness of their conduct. Finally, Corporal Branch ordered the officers to keep Sanford (P) in restraints until stronger restraints arrived and then he left the scene. Attorneys representing the ordered officers would have a different argument than the attorney representing Corporal Branch. Plaintiffs also allege several conflicts among the MCV medical defendants. First, the assertion that Dr. Meguid misdiagnosed Sanford (P) and then failed to comply with policy when he did not caution against use of Haldol in the computer system conflicts with the arguments the other medical staff want to make about their response in light of Dr. Meguid's diagnosis. Further, the nurses had no basis to know not to use Haldol because Dr. Meguid did not follow protocol. That could eliminate the nursing staff liability. Third, CNO Crosby claimed Nurse Brown was properly trained in every respect, including the restraint policy. Nurse Brown might want to argue her actions were reasonable ones and she was not properly trained. Fourth, the operating physician was on vacation post-procedure and turned Sanford's (P) care over to another doctor. Plaintiffs make claims against the operating physician, but he is arguing he turned over all care to the covering physician. Finally, Dr. Maiberger prescribed Haldol without seeing Sanford (P) but in reliance on Nurse Brown's description of six officers holding a wild Sanford (P) down. The record does not support that version of facts because only two officers held Sanford (P) down and he was calm well before Haldol was administered. Dr. Maiberger may want to point

Continued on next page.

to Nurse Brown's inadequate description. Disqualification of counsel is a drastic step, but real conflicts such as those here require withdrawal or disqualification. The summary judgment motions and expert opinion testimony has resulted in defense positions better for the defense as a whole rather than for the interests of the individual defendants. Each defendant is entitled to use the entire record to defend himself. The lawyer representing the multiple defendants is not free to pursue a course of individual defense because that would be adverse to his other clients. Counsel for defendants argue the defendants each agreed to joint representation, but nothing indicates the detailed conflicts were presented and fully explained to the defendants. Neither attorney could request a waiver because neither reasonably could believe they could represent all these defendants under these circumstances. The counsel, once disqualified, should not remain in the case, but that will remain open for discussion after each defendant is separately advised by non-conflicted counsel. Motion granted.

▶ *ANALYSIS*

Attorneys have an obligation to provide individualized, independent advice to each client. Clients may have joint interests, but that may not permit joint representation in every instance. The burden is on the attorney to determine the appropriateness of the representation both before and during the representation. It is not the client's obligation to bring conflicts to the attorney's attention.

Quicknotes

CONFLICT OF INTEREST Refers to ethical problems that arise, or may be anticipated to arise, between an attorney and his client if the interests of the attorney, another client or a third-party conflict with those of the present client.

Anderson v. O'Brien

Elderly widow (P) v. Preying home buyers (D)

Conn. Super. Ct., 2005 Conn. Super. LEXIS 3365 (2005).

NATURE OF CASE: Motion to dismiss counts of revised complaint against attorney.

FACT SUMMARY: The O'Briens (D) persuaded Anderson (P) to sell them her home with the understanding she would live on the property in a cottage they built for her. Anderson (P) signed a purchase agreement, but the O'Briens (D) brought her to a closing one month earlier than agreed, late in the afternoon, when she was ill. She asked the O'Briens' (D) attorney, Peter I. Manko (D), if she needed her own attorney but he said she did not. He claimed to represent her, the O'Briens (D), and the lender. After the closing, the O'Briens (D) mistreated Anderson (P) and built her a barn-like structure instead of a cottage. She sued the O'Briens (D) and Manko (D).

🏛 **RULE OF LAW**
An attorney involved in joint representation owes a duty of loyalty to each individual client and cannot continue representation where a conflict exists and the client does not or cannot knowingly consent to the conflict.

FACTS: Anderson (P), a childless widow, owned a single-family residence on property in a desirable neighborhood. The O'Briens (D) befriended her to convince her to sell her property. They finally convinced her after promising to build her a cottage on the property, allowing her to stay through her lifetime, and treat her as a member of the family. Anderson (P) signed a purchase agreement prepared by the O'Briens' (D) attorney, Peter I. Manko (D). The closing date was August 1, but the O'Briens (D) unexpectedly picked her up on July 3 to take her to the closing. It was late in the afternoon and she'd been ill. Anderson (P) questioned Manko (D) if she needed independent counsel, but he assured her he was her attorney as well as representing the O'Briens (D) and the lender. Anderson (P) signed the closing documents without reviewing them or having them read to her. The O'Briens (D) then began mistreating Anderson (P). They also only built her a barn-like structure that did not fit her furnishings instead of the promised cottage. Nothing in the closing documents referenced her life estate in the cottage although a clause did mention the cottage. Anderson (P) sued the O'Briens (D) and Manko (D) on a number of counts. Manko (D) moved to dismiss the counts against him.

ISSUE: Does an attorney involved in joint representation owe a duty of loyalty to each individual client and must he discontinue representation where a conflict exists

and the client does not or cannot knowingly consent to the conflict?

HOLDING AND DECISION: (Lopez, J.) Yes. An attorney involved in joint representation owes a duty of loyalty to each individual client and cannot continue representation where a conflict exists and the client does not or cannot knowingly consent to the conflict. Anderson (P) properly alleged a claim for legal malpractice, but Manko (D) claims the allegations do not lead to a proper claim for recklessness. The plaintiff alleges Manko (D) knew or should have known of her illness, that she needed separate counsel, that he failed to prepare a deed subject to her life estate so the lender's interest was superior to hers, and Manko (D) did not treat Anderson (P) as his own client. The actions arise to recklessness beyond mere malpractice. Anderson (P) also alleges Manko (D) violated the Connecticut Unfair Trade Practices Act (CUTPA) by his representation of the seller, purchaser, and lender in the same transaction. The court must consider the "cigarette rule" set out by the Federal Trade Commission to determine the unfairness of an act if it offends public policy, is immoral, and causes substantial injury to consumers. The Rules of Professional Conduct set forth what offends public policy as it relates to attorney actions, and Manko's (D) actions seem to violate one of the Rules, so the first prong of the cigarette test is met. The allegations, if proven, satisfy the second and third prongs. Finally, Manko (D) argues that not all professional negligence is a breach of fiduciary duty. Manko (D), however, owed a duty of loyalty to his client, Anderson (P), when he assured her he was her attorney and she could rely on him in the closing. His failure to look to her best interests, if proven, would be a breach of his duty to her. Motion denied.

▶ **ANALYSIS**

Attorneys in joint representation situations have to tread lightly and remember that it is difficult, if not impossible, to see to each individual client's best interests if those interests might diverge. Complete disclosure, informed consent, and written consent are absolute requirements in joint representations.

■≡■

Quicknotes

BREACH OF FIDUCIARY DUTY The failure of a fiduciary to observe the standard of care exercised by professionals of similar education and experience.

Continued on next page.

DUTY OF LOYALTY A director's duty to refrain from self-dealing or to take a position that is adverse to the corporation's best interests.

MALPRACTICE A failure to perform one's professional duties during the course of a client relationship, either intentionally or negligently; or the poor or improper discharge of one's professional obligations.

MOTION TO DISMISS Motion to terminate an action based on the adequacy of the pleadings, improper service or venue, etc.

NEGLIGENCE Conduct falling below the standard of care that a reasonable person would demonstrate under similar conditions.

A. v. B.

[Parties not identified.]

N.J. Sup. Ct., 726 A.2d 924 (1999).

NATURE OF CASE: Appeal of paternity action joining law firm as third-party defendant.

FACT SUMMARY: Husband and Wife engaged Hill Wallack law firm to prepare estate planning documents leaving their respective estates to each other. Husband fathered an illegitimate child but did not inform Wife or his estate lawyer. Mother of the illegitimate child coincidentally hired a family law attorney with Hill Wallack to represent her in a paternity action against Husband. When the conflict was discovered, Hill Wallack withdrew from representation of Mother and informed Husband it intended to disclose the child's existence to Wife. Husband named Hill Wallack as a third-party defendant in the paternity action to prevent disclosure.

🏛 RULE OF LAW
A law firm may disclose confidential information of one co-client to another co-client if fraud is at issue and the parties implicitly or expressly agreed to share information.

FACTS: Husband and Wife engaged Hill Wallack, a sixty-member law firm, to prepare their estate planning documents. Husband and Wife signed an engagement letter titled "Waiver of Conflict of Interest" which explained information provided by each could become available to the other. Each intended to leave his or her estate to the other with the residuary potentially inherited by issue, legitimate or illegitimate. Prior to executing the wills, Husband fathered a child outside of the marriage with Mother. He agreed to take a paternity test but could not agree on child support. Mother coincidentally hired Hill Wallack to represent her in a paternity action against Husband. The estate planning file and computer system misspelled Husband and Wife's last name due to a clerical error, so the family law attorney did not learn of the conflict when he correctly input Husband's last name into the conflict check system. Husband and Wife executed the wills. The estate attorney remained unaware of the family law attorney's representation of Mother against Husband until Husband's attorney in the paternity action informed Hill Wallack it already had Husband's assets information. Hill Wallack immediately withdrew from representation of Mother. Hill Wallack sent a letter to Husband informing Husband that it had an ethical obligation to disclose the child's existence to Wife because she remained unaware that her estate could potentially go to the child, which was a material fact affecting her estate planning. Husband then named Hill Wallack as a third-party defendant in the paternity

action and requested the court prohibit Hill Wallack from disclosing the child's existence to Wife.

ISSUE: May a law firm disclose confidential information of one co-client to another co-client if fraud is at issue and the parties implicitly or expressly agreed to share information?

HOLDING AND DECISION: (Pollock, J.) Yes. A law firm may disclose confidential information of one co-client to another co-client if fraud is at issue and the parties implicitly or expressly agreed to share information. A conflict here arises out of the firm's duty of confidentiality to each client as well as its duty to inform clients of material facts. Hill Wallack argues it is mandatory to disclose the child's existence because it reasonably believes disclosure is necessary to avoid a fraud on Wife. The facts do not support mandatory disclosure because the child's potential inheritance is too remote. Permissive disclosure is appropriate, however. The facts support the allegation that Husband used Hill Wallack to defraud Wife in her estate preparation because she is unaware of a child that could be entitled to a majority of Husband's estate and possibly inherit her own. Further, the Conflict of Interest waiver implicitly states the co-clients will have access to confidential information of the other, thus permitting the disclosure. Legal research reveals comments and other states' evaluations of somewhat similar situations that permit disclosure. It is preferable to have a disclosure agreement in joint representation which clearly outlines client's expectations of confidentiality from the co-client. Disclosure is inappropriate where one client expressly precedes confidences with a mandate for confidentiality or where co-clients reasonably expect some things will be kept confidential. Here, Husband did not actually communicate anything to the firm because Hill Wallack learned of the child's existence through a third party. Also, the parties at least implicitly agreed to share confidential information. Finally, this state's professional rules permit disclosure to rectify a fraudulent situation. Hill Wallack may inform Wife of the existence of the child.

▶ ANALYSIS

Written agreements and consents are vital to joint representation. Attorneys should be careful to make full disclosure of what joint representation will entail, including sharing of confidential information with co-clients. Clients can limit the joint representation as needed, in writing, or can freely waive confidentiality as to co-clients. A primary

Continued on next page.

focus of this case was the agreement initially signed by Husband and Wife permitting disclosures, so the importance of a writing cannot be overstated.

■━■

Quicknotes

JOINDER OF PARTIES   The joining of parties in one lawsuit.

■━■

Eastman Kodak Company v. Sony Corporation

Acquiring company (P) v. Alleged patent infringer (D)

2004 U.S. Dist. LEXIS 29883 (W.D.N.Y. 2004).

NATURE OF CASE: Motion to disqualify.

FACT SUMMARY: Woods Oviatt Gilman LLP (Woods Oviatt) defended its long-time client, Heidelberg Digital LLC, in two employment discrimination cases. During the litigation process, Eastman Kodak Company (Kodak) (P) acquired Heidelberg. Woods Oviatt subsequently accepted representation of plaintiffs in a class action case and Sony Corporation (D) in the patent infringement case with Kodak (P) as the opposing party in both. Kodak (P) moved to disqualify Woods Oviatt based on conflict of interest.

🏛 RULE OF LAW
A subsequently acquired entity may be considered the same entity as the acquiring entity for conflict of interest purposes requiring disqualification of counsel representing interests adverse to the newly created entity.

FACTS: Woods Oviatt Gilman LLP (Woods Oviatt) had a long history of avoiding Eastman Kodak Company (Kodak) (P) as a client so it could represent those entities and persons with adverse interests. Woods Oviatt's long-time client, Heidelberg Digital, LLC (Heidelberg), was a defendant in two employment discrimination cases and Woods Oviatt was heavily involved in the defense of both cases. One case alleged Heidelberg racially discriminated against an African-American employee. Kodak (P) acquired Heidelberg. Woods Oviatt was instructed to continue representation of Heidelberg-now-Kodak in the discrimination cases. Subsequent to the acquisition, Woods Oviatt accepted representation of two new clients, a class of plaintiffs in an employment discrimination suit against Kodak (P) and Sony Corporation (D) in its defense against Kodak's (P) claim of patent infringement. Kodak (P) claimed the existence of a conflict now that it was a client of Woods Oviatt through its acquisition of Heidelberg and refused to execute a waiver. Woods Oviatt offered to withdraw from the employment discrimination cases, but Kodak (P) claimed that would unfairly prejudice them. Kodak (P) moved to disqualify Woods Oviatt as local counsel for the class plaintiffs and Sony (D).

ISSUE: May a subsequently acquired entity be considered the same entity as the acquiring entity for conflict of interest purposes requiring disqualification of counsel representing interests adverse to the newly created entity?

HOLDING AND DECISION: (Feldman, J.) Yes. A subsequently acquired entity may be considered the same entity as the acquiring entity for conflict of interest pur-

poses requiring disqualification of counsel representing interests adverse to the newly created entity. First, the court must determine if Heidelberg and Kodak (P) are now a single entity for conflict purposes. The facts support such a finding because Kodak (P) basically subsumed Heidelberg rather than merged as an equal. Next, does representation of the newly single client constitute a prime facie conflict? Essentially, the existing client, Kodak (P), is now an adverse party in the two new cases, so an unacceptable conflict exists. Third, the court must consider whether the conflict requires disqualification. Kodak (P) refuses to consent to waive the conflict so Woods Oviatt must show that the representation of the clients will not suffer due to the conflict of loyalties. Woods Oviatt cannot make such a showing here. Its employment discrimination case is defending now-Kodak (P) against a claim by an African-American former employee that Kodak (P) discriminates against African-Americans. Woods Oviatt's class of plaintiffs are claiming Kodak (P) discriminates against African-Americans; the adverse party in the first discrimination case could very well qualify as a class plaintiff in the second. Disqualification is necessary here, but the court must determine whether Woods Oviatt is disqualified from acting as Kodak's (P) counsel or as counsel in the two new cases. Kodak (P) argues that the "hot potato principle" should apply here where Woods Oviatt cannot abandon its current client for a "better, more attractive" client. Woods Oviatt argues for a more flexible approach because the conflict arose out of the business activities of its client rather than any overt act of Woods Oviatt. The court favors the flexible approach, but under either approach, Woods Oviatt must be disqualified from the new representation. Applying the *Gould* factors, 738 F. Supp. 1121 (N.D. Ohio 1990), Kodak's (P) concern over the sharing of confidential information is understandable, the cost and inconvenience in obtaining new representation in the employment discrimination cases is significant, and Woods Oviatt was aware Kodak (P) had acquired Heidelberg when it accepted representation of the new clients. It may be fairer for Kodak (P) to waive the conflict, but Woods Oviatt must be disqualified from representation of clients with interests adverse to Kodak (P). This does not apply to future clients after Woods Oviatt concludes representation in the employment discrimination; this court will look askance at any Kodak (P) claim that Woods Oviatt owes it further loyalty as a "former" client. Kodak (P) cannot use its status as a litigation tactic in future cases. Motions granted.

Continued on next page.

▶ *ANALYSIS*

While most attorneys are aware of the basic rule that one cannot represent both adversaries, the identity of the parties involved can be a more complex question. Here, the business decision of the client resulted in the disqualification of a law firm from two potentially lucrative and successful claims. Woods Oviatt would have been well-advised to seek and obtain Kodak's (P) conflict waiver for future cases after its acquisition of Heidelberg and prior to accepting new representation.

∎▬∎

Quicknotes

EMPLOYMENT DISCRIMINATION Unequal treatment of individuals in respect to the conditions of their employment, or in the application process, without justification.

∎▬∎

Conflicts of Interest: Specific Rules

Quick Reference Rules of Law

Liggett, d/b/a Liggett Construction Company v. Young

Contractor (P) v. Attorney (D)

Ind. Sup. Ct., 877 N.E.2d 178 (2007).

NATURE OF CASE: Appeal from summary judgment in contract action.

FACT SUMMARY: Liggett (P) and the Youngs (D) contracted for Liggett (P) to construct the Youngs' (D) residence. Dean Young (D) was acting as Liggett's (P) personal lawyer on an unrelated matter. Dean Young (D) drafted and inserted a clause into the form construction contract requiring written change orders. The Youngs (D) made oral change orders. Liggett (P) sued to recover compensation for the change orders and the Youngs (D) sought to enforce the Dean Young (D) clause of the contract.

🏛 RULE OF LAW
A transaction entered into between attorney and client during the fiduciary relationship is presumptively invalid and only overcome by a showing the transaction is fair and reasonable.

FACTS: Ronald Liggett d/b/a Liggett Construction Company (Liggett) (P) filed a third-party complaint against Dean and Elisabeth Young (D) related to Liggett's (P) construction of the Young (D) residence. The Youngs (D) counterclaimed for damages alleging negligent and untimely performance under the building contract. The trial court granted partial summary judgment and entered final judgment on all counts in favor of the Youngs (D). Liggett (P) appealed.

ISSUE: Is a transaction entered into between attorney and client during the fiduciary relationship presumptively invalid and only overcome by a showing the transaction is fair and reasonable?

HOLDING AND DECISION: (Dickson, J.) Yes. A transaction entered into between attorney and client during the fiduciary relationship is presumptively invalid and only overcome by a showing the transaction is fair and reasonable. Liggett (P) argued the building contract is unenforceable because Dean Young (D) was Liggett's (P) attorney at the time he drafted the building contract for the construction of the Young (D) residence. He contends Indiana Professional Conduct Rule 1.8 restricts an attorney's ability to engage in transactions with his client and governs the relationship here. The Youngs (D) argued Rule 1.8 does not apply to the contract because standard commercial transactions are excepted. Liggett (P) offers building services to the public and that is the basis of the contract with the Youngs (D). Whether or not Rule 1.8 applies, Dean Young (D) owed his client a fiduciary duty and transactions entered into during the fiduciary relationship are presumptively invalid. The construction contract here was a standard pre-printed form, but Dean Young (D) drafted and inserted a clause requiring written change orders. The Youngs (D) acknowledge Dean Young (D) was acting as Liggett's (P) attorney on an unrelated matter when the parties entered into the construction contract. The Youngs (D) did not meet their burden to demonstrate the building contract was fair and reasonable so as to overcome the presumption of invalidity. The Youngs (D) are not entitled to partial summary judgment of Liggett's (P) claims against them. Remanded.

CONCURRENCE: (Boehm, J.) Liggett's (P) claim is for compensation for oral change orders. Summary judgment for the Youngs (D) should be reversed. This plainly is not a "standard" contract contemplated by the exception to Rule 1.8. That is intended for truly "standard" transactions such as phone service for a lawyer who represents the telephone company. In no case should the attorney draft the service contract. Dean Young (D) prepared a contract clause requiring change orders in writing. Then the Youngs (D) made oral change order requests and now seeks to enforce the clause Dean Young (D) drafted. That, on its face, is not "fair and reasonable" to the contractor. The resulting loss should be in the lawyer's lap, not the client's. Liggett (P) is entitled to recover the fair compensation attributable to the changes.

▶ ANALYSIS

It is permissible but not recommended for attorneys to engage in business relationships with clients. At times, it cannot be avoided, which is why many professional conduct rules permit standard transactions. When it is a voluntary undertaking, however, the attorney has the burden to protect the client and ensure the relationship does not favor the attorney to the detriment of the client.

Quicknotes

FIDUCIARY DUTY A legal obligation to act for the benefit of another, including subordinating one's personal interests to that of the other person.

Burrow v. Arce

Plaintiff's attorney (D) v. Unidentified party (P)

Tex. Sup. Ct., 997 S.W.2d 229 (1999).

NATURE OF CASE: Appeal from grant of summary judgment.

FACT SUMMARY: David Burrow (D) and his firm filed a personal injury suit on behalf of 126 plaintiffs and negotiated a settlement. Each plaintiff received a set amount regardless of injury or individual factual circumstances. The total settlement was for $190 million and the attorneys took a $60 million contingency fee. Forty-nine of the former plaintiffs filed suit against Burrow (D) and his firm for breach of fiduciary duties and sought disgorgement of all fees Burrow (D) received.

RULE OF LAW
Fee forfeiture is an appropriate remedy despite the lack of actual damages to the client but the amount of forfeiture and for what misconduct are questions for the court to determine.

FACTS: David Burrow (D) and several attorneys in his firm (Attorneys) filed a personal injury suit on behalf of 126 plaintiffs regarding an explosion at a Phillips 66 chemical plant. Multiple other attorneys represented numerous other injured parties in personal injury and wrongful death lawsuits arising out of the same explosion. The Attorneys (D) negotiated a $190 million settlement for the plaintiffs. $60 million of the settlement was paid to the Attorneys as a contingency fee. Forty-nine former plaintiffs (Clients) filed suit against the Attorneys (D) for breach of fiduciary duty and sought disgorgement of the $60 million. At trial, the Clients testified they only individually met with the attorneys for 20 minutes, they signed blank engagement forms that later had 33⅓ percent filled in as the contingency fee when they were orally promised 25 percent, they were coerced into settlement, and the settlement was in the aggregate with no consideration given to level of injury or particular circumstances of the individual plaintiffs. The Attorneys (D) testified that they did not settle in the aggregate, plaintiffs received a fair settlement, these plaintiffs were unhappy after hearing rumors of other settlement payments to plaintiffs represented by other attorneys, another attorney offered to represent the Clients against the Attorneys for a nominal fee and ⅓ of any recovery which led to this suit as extortion of greater sums than the agreed-upon settlement amount. The district court granted the Attorneys (D) summary judgment on the basis that the Clients suffered no actual damages because the settlement was fair and reasonable and therefore disgorgement of fees was not appropriate. Plaintiffs appealed.

ISSUE: Is fee forfeiture an appropriate remedy despite the lack of actual damages to the client but the amount of forfeiture and for what misconduct questions for the court to determine?

HOLDING AND DECISION: (Hecht, J.) Yes. Fee forfeiture is an appropriate remedy despite the lack of actual damages to the client but the amount of forfeiture and for what misconduct are questions for the court to determine. The Clients argue disgorgement is appropriate whether they were actually damaged or not and that their lack of actual damage has not been proven as a matter of law. The Attorneys (D) argue fee forfeiture is inappropriate where no actual damage is suffered and should not be ordered anyway for the breaches alleged here. The Attorneys (D) failed to establish a lack of actual damages as a matter of law, so summary judgment was not appropriate. The issue then becomes the fee forfeiture. Actual damages are not necessary for fee forfeiture to occur because fee forfeiture serves as an incentive for an attorney to abide by his fiduciary duty as well as a deterrent to an attorney contemplating breach. Fee forfeiture punishes the attorney's disloyalty rather than compensates the client for the actual damages, so proof of actual damages is not necessary. Despite the Attorneys' (D) claim, no evidence exists that plaintiffs routinely attempt to extort additional monies from attorneys without a requirement for proof of actual damages. The Clients are not correct, however, in arguing all misconduct requires a complete fee forfeiture. That would put too heavy a burden on an attorney to account for each inadvertent misstep by disgorging fees for years of appropriate, successful work. This court disagrees with the Restatement of Law proposition that fee forfeiture should be total. The amount of forfeiture should be determined on a case-by-case basis taking into account the willfulness of the violation, the effect on the client, adequacy and availability of other remedies, and the public's interest in the integrity of the judicial system. The ultimate decision for the amount of forfeiture, whether partial or total, rests with the court. A jury will adjudicate factual issues, such as when misconduct occurred, before the court will consider whether the misconduct was a clear and serious violation of duty as well as whether and how much forfeiture is appropriate. The court's decision is then subject to appeal. Reversed.

ANALYSIS

While courts are certainly interested in compensating individuals for undeserved losses, the courts must focus on maintaining the integrity of the judicial system. The disgorgement of fees or other benefit received is not so much compensation to the client for losses suffered but a

Continued on next page.

sanction to the attorney for violating the public trust in breaching fiduciary duties. The court here does not address the burden of proof for a fee forfeiture case, but presumably the burden is first on the client to prove the violation and then shifts to the attorney to justify an award less than full forfeiture.

■===■

Quicknotes

BREACH OF FIDUCIARY DUTY The failure of a fiduciary to observe the standard of care exercised by professionals of similar education and experience.

FIDUCIARY DUTY A legal obligation to act for the benefit of another, including subordinating one's personal interests to that of the other person.

SUMMARY JUDGMENT Judgment rendered by a court in response to a motion made by one of the parties, claiming that the lack of a question of material fact in respect to an issue warrants disposition of the issue without consideration by the jury.

■===■

Iowa Supreme Court Attorney Disciplinary Board v. Monroe

Attorney disciplinary agency (P) v. Attorney (D)

Iowa Sup. Ct., 784 N.W.2d 784 (2010).

NATURE OF CASE: Attorney disciplinary action.

FACT SUMMARY: Monroe (D) represented Doe and began a sexual relationship with her that lasted several weeks.

🏛 RULE OF LAW
An attorney cannot have a sexual relationship with a client unless that client is the attorney's spouse or the sexual relationship predated the initiation of the client relationship.

FACTS: William Monroe (D) began representing Doe in early spring 2007 in a dissolution action. By late May 2007, he and Doe voluntarily began a sexual relationship. Monroe (D) later represented Doe in resolving criminal charges against her. The parties ended their relationship by mutual agreement in late August 2007. Doe's husband learned of the relationship, informed his attorney, and the attorney reported Monroe (D) to the Iowa Supreme Court Attorney Disciplinary Board (the "Board") (P). Monroe (D) withdrew from the dissolution case but continued to represent Doe in the criminal charges. Doe testified she voluntarily entered the relationship, did not feel pressured, and remained friends with Monroe (D) before, during, and after the relationship. She did ask Monroe (D) to stop contacting her new attorney in the dissolution case because she was billed for those conversations. The Board (P) filed charges against Monroe (D).

ISSUE: Can an attorney have a sexual relationship with a client?

HOLDING AND DECISION: (Ternus, C.J.) No. An attorney cannot have a sexual relationship with a client unless that client is the attorney's spouse or the sexual relationship predated the initiation of the client relationship. Monroe (D) does not appear to understand the ethical violation here. He argued his representation of Doe on the public intoxication case was proper because the sexual relationship predated his representation of Doe on that matter. Rule 1.8(j) prohibits sexual relationships with clients unless the client is a spouse or the relationship predates the initiation of the lawyer-client relationship. There is no standard sanction for this misconduct. A suspension is warranted due to the nature of the ethical infraction and the need to deter similar behavior in other attorneys. The ethical violation is clear and there is no gray area when an attorney engages in an intimate relationship with his client. This type of misconduct jeopardizes the client's interests. It is an aggravating circumstance when the client is in a dissolution proceeding and it is possible it could affect child custody proceedings. Doe was a vulnerable client because of the dissolution proceedings and because she was experiencing situational depression. In mitigation, this is not the more egregious case considered. Monroe (D) had not engaged in misconduct in the past, Doe did not feel Monroe (D) took advantage of her, and Doe appears not to have suffered emotional harm. The only apparent harm here may have been the bill for the conversations between Monroe (D) and Doe's new dissolution attorney. Monroe (D) needs a better understanding of his ethical obligations and the impact of his behavior on vulnerable clients. Without that understanding, he is a risk to the public. He has, however, been in therapy and his therapist has filed a report that he understands the power dynamics and the consequences of his behavior. Monroe (D) does not need to undergo additional counseling prior to applying for reinstatement. Monroe (D) suspended for thirty days.

▶ ANALYSIS

The attorney-client relationship requires the attorney to always act in the best interests of the client. Many clients are vulnerable and undergoing emotional turmoil when an attorney is necessary. Initiating a sexual relationship with a client during representation ignores the client's best interests and places the fiduciary relationship at risk. The professional conduct rules recognize discrete situations an intimate relationship may exist, but there are no further exceptions.

■=■

Quicknotes

ETHICS Of or relating to moral action, conduct, motive or character; professionally right or befitting; conforming to professional standards of conduct.

■=■

Paradigm Insurance Co. v. The Langerman Law Offices, P.A.

Insurance company (P) v. Law firm (D)

Ariz. Sup. Ct., 24 P.3d 593 (2001).

NATURE OF CASE: Appeal from the reversal of a defense summary judgment.

FACT SUMMARY: When Langerman (D) was sued for legal malpractice by Paradigm Insurance Co. (Paradigm) (P) which had hired him to defend one of its insureds, Langerman (D) argued that since there was no express agreement that he also represented Paradigm (D), he had no attorney-client relationship with Paradigm (D) on which Paradigm (D) could base its suit.

> **RULE OF LAW**
> An express agreement is not a prerequisite to the formation of an attorney-client relationship.

FACTS: Paradigm Insurance Co. (Paradigm) (P) issued an insurance policy covering a physician for medical malpractice liability. The physician was sued for malpractice, and Paradigm (P) hired an attorney, Langerman (D), to defend the case. Langerman (D) failed to perform certain investigations regarding the case which were vital to a competent defense. Furthermore, Paradigm (P) subsequently learned that Langerman (D) had undertaken representation of a claimant who was bringing an action against another Paradigm-insured physician. The latter representation violated an agreement between Paradigm (P) and Langerman (D) that the latter would not represent any claimants against Paradigm's (P) insureds. Paradigm (P) brought suit against Langerman (D) for malpractice. On summary judgment, the trial judge held that because there was no express agreement that Langerman (D) could represent both Paradigm (P) and the physician whom Paradigm (P) insured, no attorney-client relationship existed between Langerman (D) and Paradigm (P), hence Langerman (D) owed no duty of care to Paradigm (P) and could not be held liable for negligence that injured only Paradigm (P) but not Langerman's (D) sole client, the insured physician. The court of appeals reversed, holding that here there was a dual attorney-client relationship. Langerman (D) appealed.

ISSUE: Is an express agreement a prerequisite to the formation of an attorney-client relationship?

HOLDING AND DECISION: (Feldman, J.) No. An express agreement is not a prerequisite to the formation of an attorney-client relationship. Quite to the contrary, a relationship of client and lawyer arises when a person manifests to a lawyer the person's intent that the lawyer provides legal services for the person and the lawyer manifests to the person consent to do so. Indeed, either intent or acquiescence may establish the relationship. As a practical matter, an attorney is deemed to be dealing with a client, as here, when it may fairly be said that because of other transactions an ordinary person would look to the lawyer as a protector rather than as an adversary. Thus, a purported client's belief that the lawyer was their attorney is crucial to the existence of an attorney-client relationship so long as that belief is objectively reasonable. The instant case presents the typical situation found when defense is provided by a liability insurer as part of the insurer's obligation to provide for the insured's defense, which includes the power to select the lawyer that will defend the claim. However, the fact the lawyer is chosen, assigned, and paid by the insurer for the purpose of representing the insured does not automatically create an attorney-client relationship between the insurer and lawyer. Here, in the absence of a conflict, the attorney, Langerman (D), has two clients, the insurer Paradigm (P) and the insured. Here, Paradigm (P) is in some ways dependent upon the lawyer it hired on behalf of its insured. For example, Paradigm (P) depended on the lawyer to represent the insured zealously so as to honor its contractual agreement to provide the defense when liability allegations were leveled at the insured. In addition, Paradigm (P) depended on Langerman (D) to thwart claims of liability and, in the event liability was found, to minimize its damages. Thus, Langerman's (D) duties to the insured were discharged for the full or partial benefit of the nonclient Paradigm (P). Affirmed.

> **ANALYSIS**

As noted in the *Paradigm* decision, most jurisdictions which have addressed the issue permit the lawyer to represent both the insurer and insured in the absence of a conflict of interest, and some jurisdictions regard both the insurer and the insured as clients of the lawyer even absent an express agreement. All jurisdictions recognize that lawyers for the insured owe at least some obligations to the insurer. Neither the Model Rules nor the Restatement takes a position on the question of whom the insurance defense lawyer represents.

Quicknotes

ATTORNEY-CLIENT RELATIONSHIP The confidential relationship established when a lawyer enters into employment with a client.

Conflicts of Interest: Former, Prospective, Imputed, and Government Clients

Quick Reference Rules of Law

Oasis West Realty, LLC v. Goldman

Developer (P) v. Former attorney (D)

250 P.3d 1115 (Cal. 2011).

NATURE OF CASE: Damages claim for breach of fiduciary duty.

FACT SUMMARY: Goldman (D) represented Oasis West Realty, LLC (Oasis) (P) in proceeding with the Hilton project. Prior to city council approval of the Hilton project, Goldman (D) and his law firm withdrew from representation of Oasis (P). Goldman (D) and his wife then actively began opposing the Hilton project.

🏛 RULE OF LAW
An attorney may not use a former client's confidential information against the client's interests even if that confidential information is not disclosed.

FACTS: In early 2004, Oasis West Realty, LLC (Oasis) (P) sought to develop its Beverly Hills property (the "Hilton project"). Oasis (P) retained the services of Kenneth A. Goldman (D) and his law firm, Reed Smith, LLP. Oasis (P) retained Goldman (D) specifically because of his connections in Beverly Hills politics and his experience in civic matters. Goldman (D) was intimately involved in the Hilton project until April 2006, when he advised Oasis (P) he and Reed Smith would no longer represent Oasis (P). Goldman (D) and his wife then actively began opposing the Hilton project. Goldman (D) began collecting signatures on a petition to put a referendum on the ballot which would allow the citizenry to overturn the Beverly Hills city council decision to approve the Hilton project. Oasis (P) retained counsel to send Goldman (D) and Reed Smith essentially a cease-and-desist letter. Oasis (P) filed suit for damages based on breach of fiduciary duty, professional negligence, and breach of contract.

ISSUE: May an attorney use a former client's confidential information against the client's interests even if that confidential information is not disclosed?

HOLDING AND DECISION: (Baxter, J.) No. An attorney may not use a former client's confidential information against the client's interests even if that confidential information is not disclosed. Oasis (P) argued Goldman (D) breached his duties to it. The elements of breach of fiduciary duty are existence of a fiduciary relationship, breach of fiduciary duty, and damages. The elements of professional negligence are (1) duty of the professional to use such skill, prudence, and diligence as other members of the profession commonly possess and exercise; (2) breach of that duty; (3) casual connection; and (4) actual loss or damage. The elements of breach of contract are (1) contract; (2) plaintiff's performance or excuse for non-performance; (3) defendant's breach; and (4) resulting damages to plaintiff. Oasis (P) contends Goldman (D)

breached his duty of loyalty and confidentiality. After the attorney-client relationship is severed, an attorney is forbidden to injuriously affect the former client or use confidential information at any time against the client. Oasis (P) asserted Goldman (D) obtained highly confidential information during his representation when he attended strategy sessions. He then used that information to actively oppose the Hilton project. It is reasonable to infer Goldman (D) did use that information and it is reasonable to infer Goldman's (D) opposition to the project developed during the representation fueled by this confidential information. Goldman (D) argued the duty to a former client applies only where the attorney has undertaken concurrent or successive representation related to the prior representation and adverse to the former client; or where the attorney disclosed confidential information. Using the former client's confidential information can be as equally damaging as disclosing the former client's confidential information. Section 125 of the Restatement Third of the Law Governing Lawyers does permit an attorney publicly to take personal positions on controversial topics without consistency with client positions, but that section is inapplicable here. Goldman (D) is not opposing a controversial policy while supporting the client's goals, but actively using Oasis's (P) confidential information to have its specific project overturned. This is not a categorical ban on attorney free speech and this situation does not require a discussion on application of imputed disqualification. Oasis (P) set forth a prima facie case of actual injury and entitlement to damages in the form of attorney fees incurred in the investigation and demand for remediation to Goldman (D) and Reed Smith. [Decision not stated in casebook.]

▶ ANALYSIS

An attorney may end the relationship with a client, but the duties to the client do not terminate with the relationship. Attorneys have an ongoing duty of loyalty and confidentiality to former clients. While free speech is protected for all citizens, attorneys essentially never have the freedom to use a client's entrusted, confidential information as the basis for the speech.

◼━◼

Quicknotes

BREACH OF CONTRACT Unlawful failure by a party to perform its obligations pursuant to contract.

Continued on next page.

BREACH OF FIDUCIARY DUTY The failure of a fiduciary to observe the standard of care exercised by professionals of similar education and experience.

PROFESSIONAL NEGLIGENCE The breach of a fiduciary duty owed to one's client, caused by the professional's actions and injurious to the client.

Cascades Branding Innovation, LLC v. Walgreen Co.

Patent licensee (P) v. Alleged infringer (D)

2012 U.S. Dist. LEXIS 61750 (N.D. Ill.).

NATURE OF CASE: Motion to disqualify in patent infringement case.

FACT SUMMARY: Cascades Branding Innovation, LLC (P) is a wholly-owned subsidiary of Cascades Ventures. Defendant Best Buy retained Robins Kaplan to represent it in the current patent infringement litigation. Cascades Ventures claimed Robins Kaplan had confidential information about litigation strategy from prior emails exchanged with another Robins Kaplan attorney years earlier.

🏛 RULE OF LAW
Court must undertake a three-level inquiry to determine if a former or prospective substantial client relationship exists: (1) a factual reconstruction of the scope of the prior legal representation; (2) whether it is reasonable to infer confidential information allegedly given would have been given to a lawyer representing a client in those matters; and (3) whether that information is relevant to issues raised in the pending litigation against the former client.

FACTS: Anthony O. Brown wholly owns Cascades Ventures, LLC, which in turn wholly owns Cascades Branding Innovation, LLC (P). Cascades Branding (P) is the exclusive licensee of the '395 Patent and sued defendants for infringement. Defendant Best Buy retained Emmett J. McMahon from Robins Kaplan. In the summer of 2010, Brown, as owner of Cascades Ventures, approached Ronald J. Schutz of Robins Kaplan to represent it in licensing and enforcing a patent portfolio (the "Elbrus Portfolio") unrelated to this litigation. Brown and Schutz exchanged emails about the Elbrus Portfolio strategy, but did not enter into a formal attorney-client relationship. Schutz informally informed Brown via email that Robins Kaplan would not represent Cascades Ventures. Robins Kaplan formally closed the file one year later with notice to Brown. Several years ago, Schutz and McMahon represented TechSearch, LLC, which Brown co-founded and headed as President. He sold it in 2005. Schutz and McMahon helped TechSearch reach settlement or licensing agreements with at least eight companies, but none of the agreements are related to the instant litigation or the Elbrus Portfolio. Cascades Branding (P) moved to disqualify McMahon and Robins Kaplan in the instant litigation on the basis it is using confidential information learned from Cascades Ventures and Brown's litigation strategies.

ISSUE: Must the court undertake a three-level inquiry to determine if a former or prospective substantial client relationship exists?

HOLDING AND DECISION: (Leinenweber, J.) Yes. Court must undertake a three-level inquiry to determine if a former or prospective substantial client relationship exists: (1) a factual reconstruction of the scope of the prior legal representation; (2) whether it is reasonable to infer confidential information allegedly given would have been given to a lawyer representing a client in those matters; and (3) whether that information is relevant to issues raised in the pending litigation against the former client. Disqualification is a drastic measure which deprives a party of its representation of choice. An attorney for a corporate entity owes a duty of loyalty to the corporate entity rather than a particular shareholder, officer, or director. When a subsidiary has the same management group, however, the lawyer must take that into consideration for conflict purposes. The Court must first consider whether Cascades Branding (P) has any former or prospective relationship with Robins Kaplan. Cascades Branding (P) is not related in any way to TechSearch. The only link is common personnel—Brown—and that is too tenuous. Further, Cascades Ventures was seeking a new representation agreement with Robins Kaplan for the Elbrus Portfolio, so even Brown did not consider the prior TechSearch relationship to extend. Cascades Branding (P), however, is a wholly-owned subsidiary of Cascades Ventures, which did engage in discussions with Schutz and Robins Kaplan about litigation strategy. The one step of removal does not eliminate the expectation of confidentiality. The lawyer could learn linking confidential information. The current litigation is directly adverse to Cascades Branding and is thus directly adverse to Cascades Ventures also. The issue is whether Cascades Ventures had a substantial relationship with Robins Kaplan. Schutz affirmatively demonstrated in an email he had confidential information and could recall it without benefit of a file. Robins Kaplan maintained the information was not a broad litigation strategy that could apply here, but Cascades Branding (P) argued the opposite. The email reflected not only the Elbrus Patent information but an overall strategy for Cascades litigation. The Court recognizes it is depriving Best Buy of its long-time, preferred counsel and does not reach its conclusion lightly.

▶ ANALYSIS

The integration of the two corporate entities is an important consideration when evaluating the possibility of a conflict in representation. If the management or legal

Continued on next page.

departments are common, then it is more likely confidential information is shared between the entities and the lawyer must restrict his or her representation. It is beneficial to any firm or lawyer to request identification of all parent companies, subsidiaries, and affiliates for a conflict check.

■━━■

Quicknotes

CONFLICT OF INTEREST Refers to ethical problems that arise, or may be anticipated to arise, between an attorney and his client if the interests of the attorney, another client or a third-party conflict with those of the present client.

■━━■

Martin v. Atlanticare

Former employee (P) v. Former employer (D)

2011 U.S. Dist. LEXIS 122987 (D.N.J.).

NATURE OF CASE: Motion to disqualify in employment discrimination case.

FACT SUMMARY: LG was the attorney working on the defense when she left her firm. She became employed at the plaintiffs' law firm. The defendant was not informed LG was now at the plaintiffs' firm until someone saw LG's name on CM's letterhead.

RULE OF LAW
A side-switching attorney with primary responsibility for a matter is disqualified from representing the former client's adversary and that disqualification is imputed to the entire new firm.

FACTS: Shelly Martin (P) and other plaintiffs filed a collective action against former employer, AtlantiCare Regional Medical Center (ARMC), for employment discrimination and violation of labor laws regarding overtime pay. Plaintiffs (P) retained Costello & Mains, P.C. (CM). ARMC retained Morgan, Lewis and Bockius LLP (Morgan) with Richard Rosenblatt (RR) as the supervising partner supported by attorneys Lisa Grosskruetz (LG) and Prashanth Jayachandran (PJ). Morgan hired LG on November 22, 2010. LG had 23 years of experience as a labor and employment attorney for several large firms. She began working on the ARMC (D) case on November 24, 2010. Between November 24, 2010 and March 4, 2011, LG billed 108.2 hours on the ARMC (D) matter. Her work included substantive review of ARMC (D) documents, litigation strategy, emails with clients, research of relevant law, and strategy sessions with RR and PJ. RR intended for LG to have primary responsibility for the case while he retained minimal oversight and PJ was involved in another matter. On March 4, 2011, LG left Morgan and joined CM. ARMC (D) was not informed of the side-switching attorney until an ARMC individual noticed LG's name on CM letterhead. On April 15, 2011, LG left CM. ARMC (D) filed a motion to disqualify CM.

ISSUE: Is a side-switching attorney with primary responsibility for a matter disqualified from representing the former client's adversary and is that disqualification imputed to the entire new firm?

HOLDING AND DECISION: (Schneider, J.) Yes. A side-switching attorney with primary responsibility for a matter is disqualified from representing the former client's adversary and that disqualification is imputed to the entire new firm. The parties agreed LG cannot represent the plaintiffs. ARMC (D) argued the disqualification should be imputed to the entire firm of CM. New Jersey does not have per se disqualification rules because it is a "fact-sensitive

nature" to disqualify counsel. The Court must first determine if LG is disqualified under Rule 1.9. Plaintiffs (P) minimized LG's role at Morgan, but conceded she is disqualified under Rule 1.9 governing duties to former clients. The next issue is whether her disqualification is imputed to CM. Plaintiffs (P) argued LG did not have "primary responsibility" for the case while at Morgan. Rule 1.10(c)(1) prohibits an attorney with primary responsibility from being screened at her new firm. If she did not have "primary responsibility," then CM could adequately screen her, not apportion to her a fee from the case, and give adequate notice to ARMC (D). Plaintiffs (P) and LG argued she did not have "primary responsibility" while at Morgan because she was an associate reviewing "mostly irrelevant and/or discoverable documents." Her billing records contradicted that assertion and ARMC's (D) declarations provided further evidence of LG's integral defense role. RR alleged LG was intimately involved in every facet. ARMC's (D) in-house counsel confirmed LG's level of involvement. Her emails also evidenced her role. It is not necessary for an attorney to be the supervising partner to be the attorney with "primary responsibility." Further, CM did not meet its burden of demonstrating adequate screening. Compliance with Rule 1.10(c)(2) requires the screening policy to be in writing and CM conceded it does not have a written policy. CM claimed it verbally instructed its staff and LG she was not to work on or have access to the Martin (P) file. CM next relied on the fact LG left the firm, but that does not cure the imputed disqualification. CM must be disqualified because LG's conflict is imputed to the entire firm.

ANALYSIS

A screening policy prohibits an individual attorney from participating in, reviewing, or accessing a specific case, client, or matter. They used to be referred to as "Chinese walls" or "Ethical walls." Not all states require screening policies to be in writing, but most states strongly recommend it. If an attorney changes firms, the conflicts resolutions must be taken seriously and a written screening policy is strong evidence of compliance.

━■━■

Quicknotes

CONFLICT OF INTEREST Refers to ethical problems that arise, or may be anticipated to arise, between an attorney and his client if the interests of the attorney, another client or a third-party conflict with those of the present client.

━■━■

Fees and Client Property

Quick Reference Rules of Law

Matter of Fordham

State bar (P) v. Attorney (D)

Mass. Sup. Jud. Ct., 668 N.E.2d 816 (1996).

NATURE OF CASE: Appeal from a ruling for defendant in case alleging excessive fees were charged by an attorney.

FACT SUMMARY: Fordham (D), an attorney representing a client charged with driving under the influence of alcohol, allegedly charged an excessively high fee.

🏛 RULE OF LAW
In determining whether fees are clearly excessive, a court may examine the difficulty of the issues presented, the time and skill required to perform the legal service properly, and the fee customarily charged in the locality for comparable services.

FACTS: The father of an accused drunk driver hired Fordham (D), an experienced litigator in a prestigious Boston law firm, to handle the case but later refused to pay the fees charged. Bar counsel charged Fordham (D) with charging a clearly excessive fee under DR 2-106(A). Fordham (D) alleged that dishonesty, bad faith or overreaching must be shown for discipline of an attorney. The hearing committee found that Fordham's (D) fee fell within a safe harbor because an agreement existed between a client and an attorney, which protected from challenge the contention that the fee was clearly excessive. Bar counsel (P) appealed to the Massachusetts Supreme Judicial Court.

ISSUE: In determining whether fees are clearly excessive, may a court examine the difficulty of the issues presented, the time and skill required to perform the legal service properly, and the fee customarily charged in the locality for comparable services?

HOLDING AND DECISION: (O'Connor, J.) Yes. In determining whether fees are clearly excessive, a court may examine the difficulty of the issues presented, the time and skill required to perform the legal service properly, and the fee customarily charged in the locality for comparable services. The hearing committee's and the board's determinations that a clearly excessive fee was not charged were not warranted. Neither precedent nor the disciplinary rules preclude discipline even though the amount of time Fordham (D) spent to educate himself and represent his client was spent in good faith and diligence. The mandate of DR 2-106 (B), by referring to a lawyer of ordinary prudence, creates explicitly an objective standard by which fees are to be judged. Dishonesty, bad faith or overreaching need not be established for discipline to be necessary. A public reprimand is the appropriate sanction for charging a clearly excessive fee and is appropriate in this case. Reversed.

▶ ANALYSIS

The court in this case considered eight factors to ascertain the reasonableness of the fee. The first factor required examining the time and labor requirement, the novelty and difficulty of the questions involved, and the skill requisite to perform the legal service properly. Another factor considered was the fee customarily charged in the locality for similar legal services. ABA Model Rule 1.5(a) is the modern equivalent to the Model Code DR 2-106(B).

Quicknotes

PUBLIC REPRIMAND An official warning or admonition.

SAFE HARBOR A tax code provision safeguarding the taxpayer from liability in respect to the payment of taxes, so long as he has made an effort to comply with the provisions of the code.

In re Everett E. Powell, II

Attorney in contingent fee case (D)

953 N.E.2d 1060 (Ind. 2011).

NATURE OF CASE: Attorney disciplinary action involving contingent fee.

FACT SUMMARY: T.G. was a vulnerable client who wanted to dissolve the special needs trust set up to prevent her dissipation of the trust assets. Ross agreed to resign as Trustee if Respondent would take over as successor trustee. Respondent accepted the position, terminated the trust pursuant to T.G.'s request, and accepted 1/3 of the trust funds as a contingent fee. He did very little work and it was an uncontested matter.

🏛 **RULE OF LAW**
An attorney should renegotiate the contingent fee when it appears in the totality of the circumstances the original contingent fee is unreasonable and excessive.

FACTS: Mark E. Ross represented T.G. in obtaining a settlement of a personal injury action. T.G. had a history of drug and alcohol abuse and was involved in an abusive relationship with J.S., the father of her six children. Ross helped T.G. set up a special needs trust to hold $42,500 of her settlement funds. The intent was to avoid pressure from J.S. and others to spend the money. Ross could not find another qualified individual or entity to serve as trustee, so he agreed to serve. T.G. began demanding the trust money. Ross sent her several letters reminding her why the trust was in place; he believed J.S. was pressuring her. Ross informed T.G. he was close to resigning and encouraged her to contact smaller banks to take over as trustee. T.G. and J.S. then consulted Everett E. Powell, II ("Respondent") (D) about accessing the trust funds. Respondent (D) suggested he take the case on contingency and the parties agreed he would provide T.G. legal services concerning removing Ross as trustee in exchange for 1/3 of the trust funds. The agreement also stated T.G. was aware the agreement could result in a substantial fee for little work, the 1/3 fee was reasonable under the circumstances, T.G. had been given the option of paying hourly, and she had been unable to find legal representation for some time. The next day, Respondent faxed correspondence to Ross requesting dissolution of the trust. Ross responded with appreciation T.G. had consulted an attorney, an offer for the trust to pay for a couple of hours of legal work, and a warning about T.G. having unfettered access to the funds. The two reached an agreement that Respondent would take over as trustee. He then was appointed Successor Trustee, dissolved the trust, and accompanied T.G. to a bank branch with the termination documents. The branch refused to permit Respondent to sign anything permitting T.G. to

withdraw the funds. The two went to another branch where Respondent did not show the termination documents and executed a signature card for the trust account as the successor trustee. He later prepared an accounting. The hearing officer rejected Respondent's 1/3 fee and determined a reasonable fee was $3,000, which included 15 hours of work at $200 per hour.

ISSUE: Should an attorney renegotiate the contingent fee when it appears in the totality of the circumstances the original contingent fee is unreasonable and excessive?

HOLDING AND DECISION: (Per curiam) Yes. An attorney should renegotiate the contingent fee when it appears in the totality of the circumstances the original contingent fee is unreasonable and excessive. Circumstances may later render unreasonable a once-reasonable fee agreement. *In re Matter of Gerard*, 634 N.E.2d 51 (Ind. 1994) involved a large contingent fee paid after a largely administrative task. The hearing officer found it important the attorney did not renegotiate the fee after realizing the minimal work involved, but instead, accepted the inflated fee. The officer found it represented greedy overreaching. Here, Respondent may reasonably have believed removing Ross as trustee was a contested matter even though he reviewed the correspondence wherein Ross expressed his willingness to step aside. He may even have questioned the amount left in the trust even though he examined trust documents showing the balance. Within days, however, Respondent was aware this was a straightforward, uncontested case. It is not necessary to reduce a contingent fee each time a case turns out to be easier or more lucrative than originally contemplated. It should not, however, provide a windfall under the totality of the circumstances. Respondent violated Indiana Professional Conduct Rule 1.5(a) by collecting a clearly excessive and unreasonable fee. The following facts aggravate the conduct: (1) Respondent is not remorseful; (2) he lacks insight into his misconduct; (3) he made evasive assertions; (4) he did not fully cooperate; (5) he was indifferent to his client's vulnerability; (6) he misrepresented to Ross his intention to terminate the trust; (7) he has not made restitution. In mitigation, Respondent was newly admitted at the time of the misconduct and he had no disciplinary history. Here, Respondent was aware of his client's particular vulnerabilities and he began the dissipation of her trust funds by accepting such an unreasonable fee. Respondent suspended for 120 days without automatic reinstatement.

Continued on next page.

▶ ANALYSIS

Contingent fee contracts can be beneficial to clients who cannot afford to pay upfront or hourly fees but have a lucrative legal matter to resolve. Those clients might not otherwise be able to obtain legal representation. The contingent fee, however, is not based on the amount of work completed or the complexity of the case; it merely relates to the final dollar amount. Attorneys bear the risk of a case becoming significantly more expensive or complex than originally thought, but clients should not pay an attorney a windfall when a simple case yields extraordinary results through little input or talent by the attorney.

■■■

Quicknotes

CONTINGENCY FEE AGREEMENT A fee agreement between an attorney and client that is dependent upon the ultimate disposition of the case and comprises a percentage of the party's recovery.

TOTALITY OF THE CIRCUMSTANCES TEST Standard, which focuses on all the circumstances of a particular case, instead of individual factors.

■■■

In re Sather

Disciplined attorney (D)

Colo. Sup. Ct., 3 P.3d 403 (2000).

NATURE OF CASE: Attorney discipline proceeding.

FACT SUMMARY: Larry Sather (D) accepted a "nonrefundable" retainer, which he spent rather than placing it in a trust account. He did not earn the entire retainer but failed to promptly return the balance to the client. The disciplinary commission recommended sanctions.

🏛 RULE OF LAW
An attorney may accept an advance, or retainer, fee but the money must remain in a trust account and is fully refundable if unearned.

FACTS: Larry Sather (D) agreed to represent Franklin Perez in a lawsuit against the Colorado State Patrol. Sather (D) prepared a fee agreement which stated Perez must pay a "minimum fee" of $20,000 which was "nonrefundable" under any circumstances, even if Perez terminated the relationship. Perez paid the fee in two installments and Sather (D) almost immediately spent the funds. Sather (D) filed the suit and the Colorado State Police offered $6,000.00 to settle. Perez rejected the settlement offer. In an unrelated matter, Sather (D) was suspended from the practice of law for thirty days. After receiving notice, Perez requested an accounting from Sather (D) but Sather (D) did not provide it. Perez terminated Sather (D) and accepted the settlement offer of $6,000.00. Sather (D) finally provided the accounting to Perez and conceded he owed Perez a refund of $13,076.36, but he did not pay any refund for two months and did not pay the full refund for five months. Approximately one year prior to accepting Perez as a client, Sather (D) had filed for bankruptcy. Perez hired an attorney to pursue a claim in bankruptcy court against Sather (D) for a refund of the paid fees. The parties later agreed to arbitration where the arbitrator awarded Perez the costs of the arbitration but no refund from the prior representation. Sather (D) did pay Perez those costs. The disciplinary commission brought charges against Sather (D) for violation of the Rules of Professional Conduct.

ISSUE: May an attorney accept an advance, or retainer, fee if the money remains in a trust account and is fully refundable if unearned?

HOLDING AND DECISION: (Bender, J.) Yes. An attorney may accept an advance, or retainer, fee but the money must remain in a trust account and is fully refundable if unearned. Sather (D) failed to keep the client's funds segregated from his funds. He testified he believed the funds were earned on receipt although he believed they were refundable. The requirement for segregation supports the theory that the funds belong to the client until they are earned by the attorney conferring a benefit on the client. The unearned funds are always fully refundable to the client upon the termination of the attorney-client relationship. If a client fears the loss of "nonrefundable funds," he may not exercise his right to end the representation. If an attorney requests an advance fee, the fee agreement must explicitly state the purpose of the fee and how/when it is earned. An attorney may charge an engagement fee, which is earned when the client retains the attorney and thus prohibits the attorney from representing an opposing party or taking on additional business. The client may also pay a retainer which protects the attorney from nonpayment after work is completed. The fee agreement here stated in very strong language that the fee was nonrefundable despite the number of hours worked. Sather (D) testified, however, that he knew the fee was refundable and treated it as such. Thus, Sather (D) knowingly misled his client and his conduct involved deceit and dishonesty. This court accepts the board's recommendation for sanction.

▶ ANALYSIS

Fee agreements, as all agreements between lawyer and client, must be clear, informative, and understood by all signing parties. In no event may a lawyer charge a nonrefundable fee, even where the fee is a "flat fee" for legal services. The fee is simply not earned until the benefit is conferred upon the client.

∎═∎

Quicknotes

ATTORNEY-CLIENT RELATIONSHIP The confidential relationship established when a lawyer enters into employment with a client.

BANKRUPTCY A legal proceeding whereby a debtor, who is unable to pay his debts as they become due, is relieved of his obligation to pay his creditors either by liquidation and distribution of his remaining assets or through reorganization and payment from future income.

SANCTIONS A penalty imposed in order to ensure compliance with a statute or regulation.

∎═∎

Malonis v. Harrington

First attorney (P) v. Second attorney (D)

Mass. Sup. Jud. Ct., 816 N.E.2d 115 (2004).

NATURE OF CASE: Review of fee dispute matter.

FACT SUMMARY: Attorney George C. Malonis (P) represented Marc J. Loiselle in a personal injury action pursuant to a contingency fee agreement. Malonis (P) performed the bulk of the litigation work and negotiated a settlement proposal. Loiselle discharged Malonis (P), however, and retained Robert W. Harrington (D) pursuant to a contingency fee agreement. Malonis (P) notified Harrington (D), Loiselle, and opposing counsel of his intent to file an attorney lien on any recovery. Harrington (D) negotiated the final settlement amount and collected his contingency fee, but did not pay Malonis (P). Malonis (P) filed suit against Harrington (D) on a quantum meruit count to recover the value of his services.

🏛 **RULE OF LAW**
Successor counsel must confer with the client prior to accepting representation and execute a written fee agreement identifying the party responsible for paying prior counsel's reasonable attorney fees and costs.

FACTS: Marc J. Loiselle retained attorney George C. Malonis (P) to represent him in a personal injury action. Malonis (P) completed the bulk of the pretrial work and entered into settlement negotiations with the defendant, Browning-Ferris Industries, Inc. (BFI). Loiselle rejected the initial settlement offers. BFI then determined to offer $57,500 although it did not communicate that offer to Malonis (P). Loiselle then discharged Malonis (P) and retained Robert W. Harrington (D) pursuant to a contingency fee agreement. Malonis (P) notified Loiselle and Harrington (D) of his intent to file an attorney lien against any future recovery. Harrington (D) wrote to Malonis (P) four times and Loiselle wrote once requesting an itemized invoice of Malonis's (P) time. Malonis (P) did not provide the requested itemization. BFI then tendered its settlement offer of $57,500, which Loiselle accepted. BFI counsel asked how Malonis (P) was going to get paid and Harrington (D) assured counsel that he would take care of Malonis (P). BFI then issued a settlement check to Loiselle and the fee check to Harrington (D) for $17,500. The same day the checks were issued, Malonis (P) sent his itemized invoice to Harrington (D) for $11,355.80. Harrington (D) thought the invoice was outrageous and paid nothing to Malonis (P). In response to Malonis's (P) demand letter, Harrington (D) refused to pay "one cent." Malonis (P) filed suit against Harrington (D) and Loiselle to recover in quantum meruit the value of his services. The trial court held Harrington (D) liable to Malonis (P) and this court transferred the case on its own motion to review the holding.

ISSUE: Must successor counsel confer with the client prior to accepting representation and execute a written fee agreement identifying the party responsible for paying prior counsel's reasonable attorney fees and costs?

HOLDING AND DECISION: (Greaney, J.) Yes. Successor counsel must confer with the client prior to accepting representation and execute a written fee agreement identifying the party responsible for paying prior counsel's reasonable attorney fees and costs. Malonis (P) performed the bulk of the services for the pretrial work required. BFI counsel testified BFI even decided to offer the $57,500 prior to Harrington's (D) involvement in the case. The record establishes Harrington (D) had accepted the responsibility to pay Malonis (P). The broader issue here is whether the client or successor counsel bears the burden of paying prior counsel for the reasonable value of his services. The discharge of an attorney discharges the client's responsibility to pay pursuant to a contingency fee agreement but the attorney is still owed the reasonable value for completed services. That may be minimal, or as in this case, for the bulk of the work. The decision must be made clearly and by specific agreement because the client cannot be asked to pay twice for the same work. Affirmed.

▶ **ANALYSIS**

Attorneys are not asked to work for free and clients are not asked to pay twice. To avoid that situation, fee agreements must be clearly understood, in writing, and executed by both parties. The successor attorney must take great care to ensure that all parties understand who is responsible for paying the prior attorney. It would benefit a discharged attorney from taking all necessary steps to ensure, in writing, who will pay his fee and when.

■=■

Quicknotes

CONTINGENCY FEE AGREEMENT A fee agreement between an attorney and client that is dependent upon the ultimate disposition of the case and comprises a percentage of the party's recovery.

LIEN A claim against the property of another in order to secure the payment of a debt.

QUANTUM MERUIT Equitable doctrine allowing recovery for labor and materials provided by one party, even though no contract was entered into, in order to avoid unjust enrichment by the benefited party.

■=■

Perdue v. Kenny A.

[Parties not identified.]

130 S. Ct. 1662 (2010).

NATURE OF CASE: Certiorari review of attorneys' fees in civil rights action.

FACT SUMMARY: Plaintiffs were successful in reforming the entire state foster-care system after years of litigation and opposition. The attorneys requested an enhanced attorneys' fee award in addition to the standard lodestar fee.

🏛 RULE OF LAW
The calculation in federal fee-shifting cases of an attorney's fee based on the lodestar may be increased due to superior performance and results.

FACTS: Plaintiffs in the action below were children in the Georgia foster-care system who filed a class-action lawsuit to reform the system. After mediation, the state and plaintiffs entered into a consent decree which reformed the entire state foster-care system and provided enforcement mechanisms. By all counts, it was an exceptional result. Respondents submitted a request for more than $14 million in attorney's fees. Half that amount was based on the lodestar calculation, i.e. the number of hours worked multiplied by the prevailing hourly rates. The other half of the requested fee was based on an enhanced award for superior work and results. The district court evaluated the request, noted the "extraordinary" results and the attorneys' "higher degree of skill, commitment, dedication, and professionalism." The district court awarded $10.5 million in fees based on a $4.5 million enhancement. [The United States Supreme Court granted writ of certiorari.]

ISSUE: May the calculation in federal fee-shifting cases of an attorney's fee based on the lodestar be increased due to superior performance and results?

HOLDING AND DECISION: (Alito, J.) Yes. The calculation in federal fee-shifting cases of an attorney's fee based on the lodestar may be increased due to superior performance and results. Congress enacted 42 U.S.C. § 1988 so a prevailing party in certain civil rights actions can recover a "reasonable attorney's fee." "Reasonable" often was left to the discretion of the trial court, which produced disparate results. The "lodestar" was developed to multiply prevailing hourly rates in the relevant market with hours spent. It is readily administrable, objective, permits judicial review, and produces reasonably predictive results. An enhanced award of fees is permissible although exceptional and rare. Section 1988 aims to enforce the civil rights statutes and the lodestar method is presumptively sufficient to accomplish this objective. The lodestar figure should include most relevant factors constituting a "rea-

sonable" fee and enhancements may not be based on factors contained within the lodestar assessment. The fee applicant must bear the burden of proving an enhancement is appropriate and prove that with "specific evidence" in support. The more favorable outcome in a case may be attributable to the superior performance of the prevailing attorneys or to the inferior performance by defense counsel or other factors. Superior results must be shown to be due to the superior attorney performance because the other reasons for a superior result cannot support an enhanced award. An enhancement may be appropriate where the hourly rate does not adequately measure the attorney's true market value; where the case required extraordinary expenses and was unusually protracted; or an exceptional delay in fee payment. This Court rejects the notion that a performance bonus may be appropriate because those cases involve reduced hourly rates. Here, the district court increased the top rate for the attorneys to more than $866 per hour without anything in the record showing that was a rate in the relevant market. The district court did address the outlay of expenses and delay in reimbursement, but did not calculate the enhancement attributable to that factor. The delay in fee payment was not outside the norm. Finally, the district court did compare the attorneys with the performance of other counsel in unnamed cases, but that does not permit meaningful review. The objectiveness of the lodestar is thus undermined. Reversed and remanded.

CONCURRENCE AND DISSENT: (Breyer, J.) An enhancement to the lodestar calculation inevitably involves an element of judgment. The plaintiffs' lawyers spent eight years developing the case and produced a record filling 20 large boxes. The district judge is aware of the many intangibles the record cannot reflect and this Court cannot easily read. The lawyers' objective here was unusually important and demanded a high degree of skill and effort. The lawsuit was lengthy and arduous. The State thoroughly opposed plaintiffs' efforts and the plaintiffs' results in the face of that opposition are exceptional. The District Judge oversaw the massive effort and evaluated the ultimate mediation and came to the conclusion the quality of service rendered by class counsel was far superior for the rates in the lodestar calculation. This is a "rare" or "exceptional" case justifying an enhancement. The judgment below should be affirmed.

▶ ANALYSIS

Each attorney fee is subject to a "reasonableness" analysis whether that fee is determined by agreement, statute,

Continued on next page.

hourly, or retroactively. Attorneys should maintain concise, detailed records of billing practices to support the reasonableness of any fee and to facilitate ongoing communication of the attorneys' efforts to clients.

■■■

Quicknotes

CERTIORARI A discretionary writ issued by a superior court to an inferior court in order to review the lower court's decisions; the Supreme Court's writ ordering such review.

■■■

CHAPTER 13

Ending the Client–Lawyer Relationship

Quick Reference Rules of Law

Gilles v. Wiley, Malehorn & Sirota

Malpractice client (P) v. Law firm (D)

N.J. Super. Ct. App. Div., 783 A.2d 756 (2001).

NATURE OF CASE: Appeal from summary judgment dismissing legal malpractice claim.

FACT SUMMARY: Denise Gilles (P) hired attorney Arthur L. Raynes with the firm Wiley, Malehorn & Sirota (D) to prosecute her legal malpractice claim. Raynes did research and obtained an expert report, but did not file the lawsuit because Gilles (P) was not promptly paying expenses. Raynes then terminated the representation just three weeks before the statute of limitations ran on Gilles's (P) case. Gilles (P) sued for legal malpractice.

RULE OF LAW

The reasonableness of withdrawal from representation is not a bright-line rule but requires consideration of the fact of representation, the sophistication of the client, the imminence of the statute of limitations, and the complexity of the case.

FACTS: Denise Gilles (P) underwent a colonoscopy on February 26, 1996 resulting in a perforation to her colon. She consulted attorney Arthur L. Raynes with the law firm Wiley, Malehorn & Sirota (D) in April 1996 to prosecute her legal malpractice claim. Raynes accepted representation and contacted an expert to evaluate her claim. The expert determined malpractice had not occurred, so Raynes confirmed with Gilles (P) if she wanted to continue and incur the additional expense to find a new expert. Gilles (P) did and Raynes obtained a favorable expert report in July 1997. Gilles (P) did not pay her expense bill and Raynes wrote her demanding payment by October 1997. Gilles (P) brought her balance down to $125 by the beginning of January 1998. The medical malpractice statute of limitations is two years, so it would run out by February 26, 1998. On January 6, 1998, Raynes wrote Gilles (P) terminating representation because Wiley, Malehorn & Sirota (D) was moving away from medical malpractice cases. His letter informed Gilles (P) of the two-year statute of limitations but did not provide a deadline date. He also provided recommendations for two medical malpractice attorneys. Gilles (P) testified she did not receive the letter until late January because she was on a trip and she did not contact any other attorney for several weeks after the statute of limitations deadline. She then filed a legal malpractice claim against Raynes and Wiley, Malehorn & Sirota (D) for unreasonably terminating representation so close to the statute of limitations deadline and for failure to reasonably protect her interests. Wiley, Malehorn & Sirota (D) moved for summary judgment and the trial court granted it, dismissing Gilles's (P) complaint. She appealed.

ISSUE: Is the reasonableness of withdrawal from representation a bright-line rule?

HOLDING AND DECISION: (Pressler, P.J.A.D.) No. The reasonableness of withdrawal from representation is not a bright-line rule but requires consideration of the fact of representation, the sophistication of the client, the imminence of the statute of limitations, and the complexity of the case. The trial court held Raynes acted reasonably based on precedent from this court approving an attorney's withdrawal just weeks prior to the statute of limitations deadline. The cases can be distinguished, however, and that prior case did not establish a bright-line rule permitting such withdrawals. Here, Raynes testified he did represent the plaintiff during the 21 months prior to termination, had all the necessary information to file the complaint for six months prior to termination, and apparently withdrew primarily because plaintiff was not promptly paying her bill for expenses. Gilles (P) was not a sophisticated litigant and did not know the critical date for the statute of limitations on her claim. Another lawyer may have reasonably needed more than three weeks to review her file and determine to accept representation, which shows that the withdrawal was unreasonably close to the deadline. Raynes took six months to review the expert report and determine her case was not as profitable as he first anticipated. An expert witness on legal malpractice opined that Raynes should have sent the termination letter by certified mail to impress upon Gilles (P) the importance of the deadline and perhaps prepare for her a pro se complaint for her to file to protect her interests. The firm cannot abandon Gilles (P) without reasonable cause or her consent. The question of the reasonableness is at least a question of fact precluding summary judgment. Reversed.

ANALYSIS

Attorneys have an obligation to disclose all material facts to clients so that clients can make fully informed decisions. The attorney in this case provided most of the facts, but failed to provide the critical date which would have allowed the plaintiff to make a fully informed, and fast, decision about proceeding with her case. The attorney had six months to review the case and decide to end representation. Procrastination is the scourge of the legal profession. Raynes should have contacted Gilles (P) significantly earlier, contacted her personally to arrange a meeting with new counsel, or prepared the pro se complaint for her to file. The obligation to the client does not

Continued on next page.

end simply because an attorney no longer has interest in the case or runs out of time to act.

■═■

Quicknotes

LEGAL MALPRACTICE Conduct on the part of an attorney falling below that demonstrated by other attorneys of ordinary skill and competency under the circumstances, resulting in damages.

PRO SE An individual appearing on his own behalf.

STATUTE OF LIMITATIONS A law prescribing the period in which a legal action may be commenced.

SUMMARY JUDGMENT Judgment rendered by a court in response to a motion made by one of the parties, claiming that the lack of a question of material fact in respect to an issue warrants disposition of the issue without consideration by the jury.

■═■

In the Matter of Steven T. Potts

Estate attorney (D)

Mont. Sup. Ct, 158 P.3d 418 (2007).

NATURE OF CASE: Attorney disciplinary action.

FACT SUMMARY: Evon Leistiko misrepresented the value of Ernestine Stukey's estate when she entered into settlement negotiations. Potts (D) knew of the misrepresentation but did nothing to correct the issue.

RULE OF LAW

An attorney has an obligation to withdraw from representation if he knows his client is engaging in fraudulent or criminal conduct.

FACTS: Ernestine Stukey (Ernestine) executed a 1998 will disinheriting her daughter, Evon Leistiko (Evon) and bequeathing most of her estate to her niece, Charlene Howard (Charlene). Ernestine and Evon had several joint accounts in which Evon was named as a beneficiary with a total of approximately $270,000.00. Ernestine's mental health deteriorated and she was involuntarily committed to hospitalization. Evon petitioned the court to be appointed Ernestine's conservator. Evon's initial inventory reported Ernestine's net worth as $1,254,795, including the joint accounts. Evon petitioned the court to distribute $160,000 in gift funds and the court denied the petition. Ernestine's attorneys alleged Evon was misappropriating and mismanaging Ernestine's funds. After investigation, Evon was removed as her mother's guardian and conservator. During that time, however, Evon moved Ernestine to an assisted living facility, and hired new counsel to draft a new will for her mother. Ernestine executed the 2001 will while staying in the Alzheimer's Unit of the facility. Ernestine died March 8, 2001, leaving Evon, six grandchildren including Tyson Leistiko (Tyson), and Charlene. A will contest ensued. Evon retained Steven T. Potts (Potts) (D) to represent her and the six grandchildren, including Tyson. Potts (D) attended the estate settlement with Evon and Tyson. Evon did not disclose she had taken possession of a fraction of the joint tenancy accounts and was working to obtain the remainder of the $270,000. Evon, Tyson, and Potts (D) did not disclose at the mediation they did not consider the joint tenancy accounts part of the estate. The parties reached an understanding and executed a Memorandum of Understanding, but did not specify a dollar figure for settlement of "the Estate." The following week, Tremper, an attorney representing Ernestine's estate, suspected Evon was attempting to secure the joint tenancy accounts and asked in writing for confirmation from Potts (D) the Estate included the accounts. Potts (D) showed the letter to Tyson who instructed Potts (D) not to respond. Potts (D) then drafted and circulated a stipulation to resolve "all" the disputes regarding Ernestine's estate as

stated in the memorandum. The parties disagreed over the meaning and effect of the stipulation and memorandum. The district court determined the parties intended the $1.2 million to be the estate total. This court affirmed and affirmed the personal representative's request to distribute the $1.2 million. The Office of Disciplinary Counsel of the State of Montana (ODC) received a complaint about Potts's (D) conduct.

ISSUE: Does an attorney have an obligation to withdraw from representation if he knows his client is engaging in fraudulent or criminal conduct?

HOLDING AND DECISION: (Judge not listed in casebook excerpt.) Yes. An attorney has an obligation to withdraw from representation if he knows his client is engaging in fraudulent or criminal conduct. Potts (D) argued his duty of confidentiality, Rule 1.6, prohibited him from discussing his clients' fraudulent behavior. Rule 1.6 provides no exception to disclose fraudulent conduct, but Rule 1.2(d) prohibits a lawyer from counseling or assisting a client in fraudulent or criminal behavior. Potts (D) also argued his clients' conduct was not fraudulent because the joint tenancy accounts passed to Evon by operation of law. The fraud was Evon's representation of the settlement value. Her conduct rose to fraud when she acted with the intent to deceive to induce another to enter into the settlement contract. Evon and Tyson both stood to benefit from the settlement agreement and did not disclose the lower value of the estate. Tyson instructed Potts (D) to suppress this relevant fact. Potts (D) argued he had no duty to correct opposing counsel's mistake, but that is inaccurate. Potts (D) did more than stay silent, he assisted his clients by drafting and circulating the stipulation knowing the other side relied on Evon's misrepresentation. Potts (D) also violated his duty of candor toward the tribunal when he did not disclose this material fact to the court. Potts's (D) actions typically justify suspension or disbarment, but there are mitigating factors here. The other parties could have demanded a specific dollar figure in the settlement agreement. A public censure is appropriate here.

CONCURRENCE AND DISSENT: (Rice, J.) The Court should have sanctioned Potts (D) with a thirty day suspension.

▶ ANALYSIS

An attorney does have a responsibility to maintain client confidentiality, but has no duty to assist a client's misconduct. The attorney may not be able to report the client's

Continued on next page.

misconduct or alert adversaries, but he can withdraw from further representation. No state requires an attorney to continue representation in cases of client misconduct.

■━━■

Quicknotes

CENSURE A statement issued by a governing body directed toward one of its members, officially reprimanding that person.

MATERIALITY Importance; the degree of relevance or necessity to the particular matter.

■━━■

Heckman v. Zurich Holding Company of America

Former in-house counsel (P) v. Former employer (D)

242 F.R.D. 606 (D. Kan. 2007).

NATURE OF CASE: Motions in retaliatory discharge action.

FACT SUMMARY: Heckman (P) worked as in-house counsel for Universal Underwriters Group (UUG) (D) and Zurich Holding Company of America (Zurich) (D). She regularly reported UUG's (D) violations and compliance audit results to upper management and directors. When the state insurance regulators learned of the violations, UUG (D) and Zurich (D) hired outside counsel. LaBeouf asked Heckman (P) to lie about the cause of the violations and she refused. UUG (D) terminated her employment.

RULE OF LAW

In-house counsel may maintain a retaliatory discharge claim against a former employee-client and may reveal only such confidential information as establishes the claim.

FACTS: Zurich Holding Company of America (Zurich) (D) hired attorney Mary Ann Heckman (P) to perform tax work for Universal Underwriters Group (UUG) (D). The UUG (D) in-house legal department was working on compliance plans because UUG (D) was significantly overcharging customers through incorrect ratings plans. UUG (D) reported its compliance plans to UUG's (D) Board of Directors, which included Zurich's (D) CEO, CFO, and CLO. Annually, UUG (D) legal department reported its violations and proposed compliance programs. Annually, UUG (D) and Zurich (D) ignored the reports and failed to implement the compliance programs. The Kansas Department of Insurance uncovered the violations and ordered UUG (D) to refund the overcharges to customers during the investigation. UUG (D) placed its general counsel on administrative leave, promoted Heckman (P) to interim general counsel, and retained outside firm LeBoeuf, Lamb, Greene and MacRae, LLP (LeBoeuf). LeBoeuf asked Heckman (P) to assert UUG (D) violations were a result of a computer glitch. Heckman (P) refused to participate in the lie, continued to report the violations and proposed compliance programs, and informed the highest Zurich (D) officers of her refusal to lie. LeBoeuf attorneys informed the state insurance regulator the violation was a result of a computer glitch. UUG (D) prohibited Heckman (P) from making statements about the investigation without running the communications through LeBoeuf. The CEO of UUG (D) assured Heckman (P) she would not be made the scapegoat. Soon thereafter, UUG (D) terminated Heckman (P) stating she failed to report the violations and requested all UUG compliance audits be suspended. UUG (D) also gave Heckman (P) a letter demanding she refrain from sharing confidential information, including with her personal attorney. UUG (D) sent an email to its employees that Heckman (P) was seeking other opportunities. All 1900 employees soon knew UUG (D) had terminated Heckman (P). Heckman (P) sued Zurich (D) and UUG (D) alleging retaliatory discharge and defamation. Zurich (D) and UUG (D) moved for judgment on the pleadings.

ISSUE: May in-house counsel maintain a retaliatory discharge claim against a former employee-client and reveal only such confidential information as establishes the claim?

HOLDING AND DECISION: (Vratil, J.) Yes. In-house counsel may maintain a retaliatory discharge claim against a former employee-client and may reveal only such confidential information as establishes the claim. Kansas courts have not considered whether in-house counsel may maintain a retaliatory discharge claim against a former employer/client. The vast majority of courts permit the claim so long as the attorney does not run afoul of her confidentiality obligation. Defendants argued the Kansas Supreme Court would not recognize the claim because of *Crandon v. State*, 897 P.2d 92 (Kan. 1995). *Crandon* notes the attorney-client relationship relies heavily on closeness and trust. The Court finds nothing in *Crandon* which would prohibit a retaliatory discharge claim. Defendants also argued such a claim does not serve public policy because attorneys must already report client misconduct. This idea has been widely rejected. Finally, defendants argued Rule 1.16 provides the client the unlimited right to terminate the attorney-client relationship. This is not, however, an unlimited right without consequence. An employee-attorney may have the rights available to other employees. Here, Heckman's (P) duty of confidentiality is shaped by Rule 1.6 and encourages the client to communicate fully and frankly. The ethical requirement of confidentiality is interpreted broadly with few exceptions. Heckman (P) may communicate just enough, however, to establish her claim to retaliatory discharge. Motion for judgment on the pleadings is overruled. Defendants are entitled to a protective order regarding the information Heckman (P) shares to establish her right to retaliatory discharge relief. Motion for protective order granted.

ANALYSIS

The attorney's duty of confidentiality is not inviolate or clients could engage in fraudulent or criminal conduct

Continued on next page.

with impunity. Clients also are not insulated from liability for engaging in discriminatory behavior towards attorney-employees. Most state courts, however, permit disclosures, even of client misconduct, under exceptionally limited circumstances.

■══■

Quicknotes

ATTORNEY-CLIENT RELATIONSHIP The confidential relationship established when a lawyer enters into employment with a client.

RETALIATORY DISCHARGE The firing of an employee in retaliation for an act committed against the employer's interests.

■══■

Pane v. Goffs

[Parties not identified.]

2009 Mass. App. Unpub. LEXIS 930; *review denied*, 914 N.E. 2d 331 (2009).

NATURE OF CASE: Appeal from dismissal of complaint in wrongful termination claim.

FACT SUMMARY: Plaintiff attorney was employed at defendant law firm when he was asked to research the law firm's obligations when inadvertently discovering possible child pornography on a client's computer. Plaintiff urged the law firm to report the images, but the law firm determined to erase them instead. Plaintiff arranged for the images to be erased but did not proceed with erasing them. The law firm terminated plaintiff's employment when the partners discovered the images remained on the computer.

RULE OF LAW
An at-will employee, including an attorney, may file a claim for wrongful termination when discharged in violation of a clearly defined public policy and reveal such confidential information necessary to support the claim.

FACTS: Plaintiff was a lawyer employed by defendant law firm. He received strong evaluations, a raise, and a merit increase during his employment. The partners asked him to research the law firm's obligations upon inadvertently discovering possible child pornography on a client or client's executive computer. Plaintiff completed the research and reported the law firm should report the finding to the authorities. The partners decided not to report the finding and instead asked plaintiff to locate an entity which could erase such images. Plaintiff urged the defendant partners to reconsider, but did locate such an entity. He did not, however, arrange for the images to be erased in the hope the partners would change their mind. Several months later, the partners discovered the images remained and terminated plaintiff's employment. He filed suit for wrongful termination in violation of public policy after reporting the images to the authorities. The court dismissed plaintiff's petition on the grounds plaintiff could not establish his case without revealing confidential information in violation of Rule 1.6.

ISSUE: May an at-will employee, including an attorney, file a claim for wrongful termination when discharged in violation of a clearly defined public policy and reveal such confidential information necessary to support the claim?

HOLDING AND DECISION: (Kafker; Graham; Wologojian, JJ.) Yes. An at-will employee, including an attorney, may file a claim for wrongful termination when discharged in violation of a clearly defined public policy and reveal such confidential information necessary to support the claim. Rule 1.6 contains limited exceptions. The trial court concluded the plaintiff could not proceed without revealing confidential information, which would require this court to determine inadvertently discovered images of possible child pornography constitute confidential information. It would also require the court to consider no exception to Rule 1.6 permits the disclosure of the law firm's investigation into its duties upon discovery of the images. This court cannot draw those conclusions from the complaint alone. The complaint does not suggest the images were related to the client's business or the underlying matter the firm was handling for the client. The complaint does not establish the images were "confidential" or "related to the representation." Further, it is not clear the images need to be "revealed." The trial court's use of protective orders and other protective devices may ameliorate confidentiality concerns. The protective orders in place already protect the client's identity. The defendant law firm assumed disclosing its investigation discussions also would reveal client secrets. Several cases have held an attorney may disclose enough information to establish the lawyer's claim in a controversy between the lawyer and a client. The plaintiff's position is similar to that of in-house counsel. There is no impediment to plaintiff revealing those facts reasonably necessary to pursue the plaintiff's wrongful termination claim. Plaintiff filed a prolix complaint and the judge was well within his discretion to strike those unnecessary portions of the complaint. [Reversed.]

ANALYSIS

An attorney must maintain client confidentiality, but there are limited exceptions when the attorney has a claim or controversy against the client or his employer. Even when the attorney has the ability to reveal confidential information, the attorney should strictly limit the disclosure to only that information necessary to support the claim or controversy.

■=■

Quicknotes

AT-WILL EMPLOYMENT The rule that an employment relationship is subject to termination at any time, or for any cause, by an employee or an employer in the absence of a specific agreement otherwise.

PROTECTIVE ORDER Court order protecting a party against potential abusive treatment through use of the legal process.

WRONGFUL TERMINATION Unlawful termination of an individual's employment.

■=■

CHAPTER 14

The Bounds of the Law

Quick Reference Rules of Law

Christian v. Mattel, Inc.

Claudene manufacturer (P) v. Barbie manufacturer (D)

286 F.3d 1118 (9th Cir. 2002).

NATURE OF CASE: Appeal from imposition of Rule 11 sanctions.

FACT SUMMARY: Harry Christian (P) retained James Hicks to file a copyright infringement claim against Mattel, Inc. (D) for allegedly infringing upon the doll head design of Christian's Claudene doll. Hicks failed to do basic investigation prior to filing the complaint which would have informed him that the allegedly offending Barbie dolls were copyrighted several years prior to the Claudene doll. Mattel (D) filed a motion seeking Rule 11 sanctions against Hicks.

RULE OF LAW

Rule 11 sanctions are limited to misconduct regarding signed pleadings, motions, and other court filings and cannot apply to other attorney misconduct.

FACTS: Mattel, Inc. (D) began designing and selling Barbie dolls in 1959. It copyrighted and marketed the Cool Blue Barbie doll in 1991. The Cool Blue Barbie dolls had a copyright notice and 1991 date stamped on the back of the doll heads. In 1996, Claudene Christian copyrighted and marketed her Claudene doll designed to resemble a University of Southern California cheerleader. Harry Christian (P) was the CFO of Claudene's company. In 1997, Mattel (D) filed a copyright infringement action against Claudene's company, which ended in a settlement. Harry Christian (P) was not a party to the settlement and he retained the same defense attorney, James Hicks, to file a copyright infringement claim against Mattel (D). Harry Christian (P) claimed the Cool Blue Barbie doll head design infringed upon Claudene's doll head design. Hicks failed to investigate the actual copyright dates prior to filing the federal complaint. Mattel (D) filed a motion for Rule 11 sanctions to be imposed on Hicks for filing a frivolous claim. Hicks ignored the motion and continued to proceed with the litigation, attempting to bury Mattel (D) in paperwork. The court granted Mattel's (D) summary judgment claim upon reviewing evidence of the doll heads' copyright dates and then granted Mattel's (D) Rule 11 motion. The court imposed sanctions on Hicks for the entire Mattel (D) legal fee amounting to $501,565.00. Hicks appealed.

ISSUE: Are Rule 11 sanctions limited to misconduct regarding signed pleadings, motions, and other court filings and cannot apply to other attorney misconduct?

HOLDING AND DECISION: (McKeown, J.) Yes. Rule 11 sanctions are limited to misconduct regarding signed pleadings, motions, and other court filings and cannot apply to other attorney misconduct. The district court noted Hicks's history of litigation abuses, his misconduct during a deposition in the instant case, his outright refusal to look at the copyright dates imprinted on the Barbie doll heads, and his outrageous tactics in filing voluminous motions and briefs. The district court found Mattel's (D) fees to be reasonable and hoped the sanctions would put an end to Hicks's misconduct. The Rule 11 sanctions, however, cannot be imposed based on misconduct outside of the pleadings, which may have occurred here. Further, the court should consider the reasonableness of Mattel's (D) claimed fees when the summary judgment argument was shockingly simple: a prior copyright cannot infringe upon a later copyright. Mattel (D) certainly needed to reply to Hicks, but did not need to use a "bazooka approach." The court must determine if Hicks had an adequate factual or legal basis to file the complaint and did he conduct an adequate investigation. The answer to both is clearly no, so Rule 11 sanctions are justified. It is the amount of fees that remains at issue. Mattel (D) argues the court can impose sanctions based on its inherent authority, which it certainly can do, but the district court did not provide that as a basis for its decision. The court must review the sanction award to determine if it applied only to the pleadings, motions, and court filings and was based on reasonable attorney fees considering the non-complexity of the issue. Vacated and remanded.

► ANALYSIS

An attorney signing a court document is personally certifying to the validity of that document. While it is not always possible to have all the facts at the time of filing the complaint, any filing attorney should have a good faith belief that the client is providing honest facts, allegations can be supported, and the claim is not frivolous. Courts do not take kindly to having their time and resources wasted. Pre-filing investigation and independent review of the client's factual allegations will provide a strong basis in the vast majority of cases for the attorney to comfortably verify a filing.

■━■

Quicknotes

COPYRIGHT INFRINGEMENT A violation of one of the exclusive rights granted to an artist pursuant to Article I, Section 8, clause 8 of the United States Constitution over

Continued on next page.

the reproduction, display, performance, distribution, and adaptation of his work for a period prescribed by statute.

PLEADING A statement setting forth the plaintiff's cause of action or the defendant's defenses to the plaintiff's claims.

SANCTIONS A penalty imposed in order to ensure compliance with a statute or regulation.

SUMMARY JUDGMENT Judgment rendered by a court in response to a motion made by one of the parties, claiming that the lack of a question of material fact in respect to an issue warrants disposition of the issue without consideration by the jury.

■━━■

Surowiec v. Capital Title Agency, Inc.

Purchaser (P) v. Escrow agency (D)

790 F. Supp. 2d 997 (D. Ariz. 2011).

NATURE OF CASE: Motion for sanctions in real estate action.

FACT SUMMARY: Surowiec (P) purchased a condominium unit and Capital Title Agency, Inc.'s (Capital's) (D) employee did not disclose the existing junior liens. When the Shamrock investors foreclosed on their junior liens, Surowiec (P) could not sell his unit and suffered financial losses. He filed a lawsuit against Capital (D), but Capital's (D) in-house counsel failed to preserve and produce documentary evidence requested by Surowiec (P).

RULE OF LAW
A party has a duty to the judicial system to preserve evidence when it knows or should know the evidence is relevant to pending or future litigation.

FACTS: James Surowiec (P) purchased a condominium unit from developer Shamrock Glen, LLC (Shamrock). Scott Romley, an employee with Capital Title Agency, Inc. (Capital) (D), acted as escrow agent. After closing, Surowiec (P) learned several Shamrock investors retained deeds of trust on the condominium unit. The investors then filed foreclosure actions and Surowiec (P) was unable to sell the property. Surowiec (P) filed a claim against Capital (D) alleging Romley knew of the encumbrances and did not tell him prior to closing. Capital's (D) in-house counsel, Lawrence Phelps (Phelps) knew of the threatened litigation and other litigation involving Shamrock investors, but he did not suspend Capital's (D) document destruction policy. He also did not accurately search for documents pursuant to Surowiec's (P) discovery requests. Surowiec (P) filed a motion for sanctions based on spoliation and discovery abuses.

ISSUE: Does a party have a duty to the judicial system to preserve evidence when it knows or should know the evidence is relevant to pending or future litigation?

HOLDING AND DECISION: (Campbell, J.) Yes. A party has a duty to the judicial system to preserve evidence when it knows or should know the evidence is relevant to pending or future litigation. Plaintiff alleged Defendants engaged in spoliation of emails and other electronic records. Surowiec (P) must prove: (1) the party having control over evidence had a duty to preserve it when it was altered or destroyed; (2) destruction or loss was accompanied by a "culpable state of mind"; and (3) the destroyed or altered evidence was "relevant" to the claims or defenses of the party seeking production. The duty to preserve arises when a party knows or should know evidence is relevant to pending or future litigation. Capital

(D) had notice of pending litigation when it received demand letters and Phelps discussed the possibility of litigation with Romley. The duty, however, is owed to the court, not to the adversary. Phelps was on notice of threatened litigation, but did not issue a litigation hold and did nothing to preserve relevant evidence. Once Capital (D) knew of pending litigation, it owed a duty to the judicial system to ensure preservation of relevant evidence. The court disagrees failure to issue a litigation hold is per se gross negligence. Here, however, Capital (D) provided no reasonable explanation for its failure to preserve. Its non-actions constituted gross negligence. The evidence here supports a reasonable inference that the failure to institute a litigation hold resulted in the loss of emails from Romley's computer related to the Shamrock development. Surowiec (P) has demonstrated the emails would be relevant and helpful to his claims because one surviving email contains very helpful information. Plaintiff has demonstrated relevance and prejudice. Courts may impose sanctions for spoliation because it is considered an abuse of the judicial process. The court must determine which sanction (1) deters parties from future spoliation; (2) places the risk of an erroneous judgment on the spoliating party; and (3) restores the innocent party to their rightful litigation place. Plaintiff sought entry of a default judgment against Defendants. There is a five-part test to determine whether a termination sanction is just: (1) the public's interest in litigation resolution; (2) docket management; (3) risk of prejudice to the moving party; (4) public policy favoring case disposition on the merits; and (5) availability of less drastic sanctions. Here, the first two factors weigh in favor and the final two factors weigh against. Plaintiff has established prejudice—the third factor—but the court cannot say he will be forced to rely on "incomplete and spotty" evidence in the face of spoliation. The factors weigh against default. Alternatively, Plaintiff sought an adverse jury instruction. That is warranted here. Motion denied as to default or preclusion, but granted as to adverse inference. Surowiec (P) also moved for sanctions for alleged discovery abuses. He claimed Capital (D) acted in bad faith by delaying searches, using improper electronic records search data, and identifying no specific documents in a "last minute data dump." Capital (D) acted willfully in filing boilerplate objections to Surowiec's (P) discovery requests and providing no documents. The conduct warrants a monetary sanction but nothing harsher. Plaintiff sought attorney's fees and costs. *Pro se* litigants, even licensed attorneys acting *pro se*, are entitled to recover fees under the court's inherent power. Capital (D) must reimburse

Continued on next page.

Plaintiff's actual expenses and reasonable attorneys' fees. Denied in part; granted in part.

▶ *ANALYSIS*

Entities should issue a litigation hold notice as soon as threatened or pending litigation is brought to the entity's attention. The litigation hold notice preserves documents and electronic information relevant to the litigation by circumventing document destruction policies and the habits of individuals to delete electronic material. Failure to implement litigation holds can result in sanctions imposed against the attorneys and the entity-party.

■━■

Quicknotes

PRO SE An individual appearing on his own behalf.

SANCTIONS A penalty imposed in order to ensure compliance with a statute or regulation.

■━■

In re Charges of Unprofessional Conduct Contained in Panel Case No. 15976

Judge (P) v. Attorney (D)

Minn. Sup. Ct., 653 N.W.2d 452 (2002).

NATURE OF CASE: Appeal from admonition to counsel for "non-serious" conduct.

FACT SUMMARY: Counsel (D) moved to exclude an obviously gainfully employed but severely disabled law clerk from the courtroom during his client's trial where the jury would be asked to award damages to his less severely disabled client for inability to work.

🏛 **RULE OF LAW**
Neither race nor disability can be used as a means to limit participation in a courtroom.

FACTS: A client was injured when a bus ran over him while he bicycled. The client was left permanently disabled and unable to work as a grocery clerk. He was uneducated and unskilled for other kinds of employment. He retained Counsel (D) to represent him in a claim for damages for future lost wages and future lost earning capacity. The judge (P) assigned to the case had one law clerk (of two working for him) who was severely disabled. The clerk was paralyzed from the mouth down, worked from a wheelchair, had a respirator, and a full-time attendant. The judge (P) assigned that clerk to this case, so the clerk would be present during the pretrial hearings, jury selection, and trial. On the first day of trial, the client expressed concern that the jury would compare the obviously gainfully employed clerk's severe disability to his lesser disability which he claimed prevented him from working and deny him the requested damages. Counsel (D) reluctantly made an oral motion for the judge (P) to exclude the clerk as potentially prejudicial to his client or to reassign the case to another judge. Counsel (D) conceded his distaste for the motion. The judge (P) denied the motion as "un-American." The jury found in favor of the defendant at trial. Counsel (D) filed a motion for a new trial based in part on the presence of the clerk in the courtroom during trial. Counsel (D) again noted his reluctance to bring up the issue. The judge (P) filed this complaint with the disciplinary commission and the Panel issued an amended admonition for the "non-serious" conduct.

ISSUE: Can race or disability be used as a means to limit participation in a courtroom?

HOLDING AND DECISION: (Per curiam) No. Neither race nor disability can be used as a means to limit participation in a courtroom. In a prior case, the disciplinary panel determined a prosecutor's conduct was "non-serious" when she requested the court exclude an African-American public defender because the public defender was allegedly being retained solely to play upon the jury's sympathy for the African-American defendant. That prosecutor realized her error, withdrew the motion, apologized to the public defenders, and initiated procedures to prevent such an error occurring again. This court disagreed with the Panel's determination that her behavior was "non-serious" because racial misconduct is inherently serious. Similarly, this court finds misconduct encompassing a person's disability to be equally serious. The facts here, however, are somewhat different. This was not Counsel's (D) prejudice toward a disabled clerk but the disabled client's rights compared to the disabled clerk's rights. Counsel (D) should have addressed the client concerns during voir dire. The clerk had the right to participate in the courtroom. The Counsel's (D) actions, however, can be properly classified as "non-serious." Affirmed.

▶ **ANALYSIS**

An attorney must balance his obligation to his client with his obligation to the court and his obligation to the public good. The counsel here should have used his litigation skills to mitigate the perceived damage caused by the presence of the disabled clerk in the courtroom when his client was claiming an inability to work. Courts cannot exclude access to a courtroom based upon race, disability, ethnicity, or other protected classes and neither can attorneys.

Quicknotes

VOIR DIRE Examination of potential jurors on a case.

Messing, Rudavsky & Weliky, P.C. v. President & Fellows of Harvard College

Law firm (P) v. College (D)

Mass. Sup. Jud. Ct., 764 N.E.2d 825 (2002).

NATURE OF CASE: Appeal from a court's sanctioning of a law firm for an ethics code violation.

FACT SUMMARY: When the law firm of Messing, Rudavsky & Weliky, P.C. (P), after initiating suit against Harvard College (D), communicated ex parte with employees of the latter, the trial court sanctioned the law firm (P) for violating a Massachusetts rule prohibiting an attorney from speaking ex parte to employees of an organization which is an adversary litigant.

🏛 RULE OF LAW
An attorney is banned from ex parte contact only with those employees of an adversary organization who have the authority to commit the organization to a position regarding the subject matter of the case.

FACTS: The law firm of Messing, Rudavsky & Weliky, P.C. (MR & W) (P) filed an employment discrimination complaint against Harvard College (D) on behalf of a woman sergeant with the Harvard University Police Department (HUPD). Following institution of the suit, the law firm (P), in further investigation of its client's case, communicated ex parte with five employees of the HUPD. It was not claimed that any of the five employees were involved in the alleged discrimination or exercised management authority with respect to the alleged discriminatory acts. The trial court granted Harvard's (D) motion to sanction MR & W (P) for violating a Massachusetts rule, adopted from the American Bar Association's Model Rules of Professional Conduct, that essentially prohibits an attorney from speaking ex parte to employees of an organization which is an adversary litigant. MR & W (P) appealed.

ISSUE: Is an attorney banned from ex parte contact only with those employees of an adversary organization who have the authority to commit the organization to a position regarding the subject matter of the case?

HOLDING AND DECISION: (Cowin, J.) Yes. An attorney is banned from ex parte contact only with those employees of an adversary organization who have the authority to commit the organization to a position regarding the subject matter of the case. The employees with whom contact is prohibited are those with "speaking authority" for the corporation, who have managing authority sufficient to give them the right to speak for, and bind, the corporation. Employees who can commit the organization are those with authority to make decisions regarding the course of the litigation, such as when to

initiate suit, and when to settle a pending case. The court recognizes that this test is a retrenchment from the broad prohibition on employee contact endorsed by the Massachusetts Rule of Professional Conduct which prohibits attorneys from communicating with a represented party in the absence of that party's attorney. We reject the lower court's interpretation of this rule in such manner that it would prohibit communications with any employee whose statements could be used as admissions against the organization pursuant to Fed. R. Evid. 801(d)(2)(D). Our test is consistent with the purposes of the rule, which are not to protect a corporate party from the revelation of prejudicial facts, but to protect the attorney-client relationship and prevent clients from making ill-advised statements without the counsel of their attorney. Prohibiting contact with all employees of a represented organization restricts informal contacts far more than is necessary to achieve these purposes. The test we here adopt protects an organizational party against improper advances and influence by an attorney, while still promoting access to relevant facts. While our interpretation of the rule may reduce the protection available to organizations provided by the attorney-client privilege, it allows a litigant to obtain more meaningful disclosure of the truth by conducting informal interviews with certain employees of an opposing organization. Reversed and remanded.

▶ ANALYSIS

As observed by the court in *Messing*, the more restrictive interpretation of the ethics rule would grant an advantage to corporate litigants over nonorganizational parties by requiring an opposing party to always seek prior judicial approval to conduct informal interviews with witnesses to an event when the opposing party happens to be an organization and the events at issue occurred at the workplace.

■■■

Quicknotes

ATTORNEY-CLIENT PRIVILEGE A doctrine precluding the admission into evidence of confidential communications between an attorney and his client made in the course of obtaining professional assistance.

EX PARTE A proceeding commenced by one party.

■■■

Disciplinary Counsel v. Stuard

State disciplinary agency (P) v. Judge (D)

Ohio Sup. Ct., 901 N.E.2d 788 (2009).

NATURE OF CASE: Disciplinary action for a judge and an attorney.

FACT SUMMARY: Judge Stuard (D) asked prosecutor Becker (D) to prepare his judicial sentencing opinion in the Roberts case. Neither Stuard (D) nor Becker (D) included Roberts' defense counsel in the discussions. Becker (D) prepared a draft opinion, Bailey (D) reviewed it and made editorial changes, and Stuard (D) accepted it as his opinion.

🏛 RULE OF LAW
Ex parte communications between a judge and an attorney appearing before that judge about the merits of the relevant case are impermissible absent the knowledge and consent of the opposing counsel.

FACTS: John M. Stuard (D) was admitted to the practice of law in 1965 and served as a judge since 1991. In 2003, Stuard (D) presided over the capital murder trial of Donna Roberts. The veteran prosecutors were Christopher D. Becker (D) and Kenneth N. Bailey (D). When the jury found Roberts guilty and recommended a sentence of death, Stuard (D) held an ex parte conference with Becker (D) and asked him to prepare the sentencing opinion. Stuard (D) gave Becker (D) pages of his notes on the aggravating and mitigating circumstances he had considered. Becker (D) agreed to draft the opinion. The next ex parte contact occurred in writing when Becker (D) provided Stuard (D) a seventeen-page draft the next day. Stuard (D) reviewed the draft, made some changes, and asked Becker (D) in a third ex parte contract to incorporate his changes. Bailey (D) reviewed the draft and made editorial suggestions. Becker (D) then incorporated Stuard's (D) and Bailey's (D) changes into a final draft. The fourth ex parte communication occurred when he provided the final draft to Stuard (D). Stuard (D) had a habit of enlisting prosecutorial assistance in drafting judicial opinions, but he failed to include Roberts' defense counsel in these communications. Defense counsel did not learn what had happened until one noticed the prosecutor silently "reading along" on a document and turning pages at the same time Stuard (D) did when Stuard (D) issued his order from the bench. Roberts's counsel objected on the basis of the impermissible collaboration and ex parte communications.

ISSUE: Are ex parte communications between a judge and an attorney appearing before that judge about the merits of the relevant case impermissible absent the knowledge and consent of the opposing counsel?

HOLDING AND DECISION: (Per curiam) Yes. Ex parte communications between a judge and an attorney appearing before that judge about the merits of the relevant case are impermissible absent the knowledge and consent of the opposing counsel. Stuard (D) conceded he violated Code of Judicial Conduct Rules 1.1 and 1.2 when he engaged in ex parte communications with Becker (D) without the consent or knowledge of opposing counsel. Becker (D) initially defended his actions but did not object to the board's report which found him in violation of Rule of Professional Conduct 8.4(d) and 3.5(b) prohibiting ex parte communications on the merits of a case and engaging in conduct prejudicial to the administration of justice. Clear and convincing evidence supports the cited misconduct. On Roberts's appeal, this court vacated and remanded the cause, with instructions for Judge Stuard (D) to personally review and evaluate the appropriateness of the death penalty. Bailey (D) merely corrected typographical errors and engaged in no ex parte communications, so the charges of misconduct against Bailey (D) are dismissed. The board considered mitigating and aggravating factors in recommending its sanctions of public reprimands. A public reprimand for both Stuard (D) and Becker (D) is appropriate.

▶ ANALYSIS

The outcome of *Stuard* may have been different had Stuard (D) and Becker (D) simply included Roberts's defense counsel in the conversations. Attorneys frequently collaborate with judges on draft opinions and rulings, but all sides must be part of the discussion. Even a quick status update can place a case in jeopardy, so it is better for judges and attorneys to talk about something other than a case on which each appears.

■=■

Quicknotes

EX PARTE A proceeding commenced by one party.

REPRIMAND An official warning or admonition.

■=■

Neumann v. Tuccio

Real estate agent (P) v. Developer (D)

2009 Conn. Super. Ct., LEXIS 2016 (2009).

NATURE OF CASE: Motion to disqualify counsel in vexatious litigation action.

FACT SUMMARY: Tuccio (D) filed a baseless complaint for slander against Neumann (P) and the court granted Neumann's (P) motion for a directed verdict. Neumann (P) then filed a vexatious litigation claim against Tuccio (D), against which Tuccio (D) argued advice of counsel.

🏛 **RULE OF LAW**
A necessary witness must have relevant and material testimony unobtainable elsewhere.

FACTS: Edward Tuccio (D), a developer-builder, filed a complaint alleging slander by Harry Neumann, Jr. (P), a real estate agent. Prior to filing, Tuccio (D) forwarded his draft complaint to the alleged witness, Robert Tuccio, Jr., who informed Tuccio (D) the statements alleged in the complaint were never made. Tuccio (D) filed and served the complaint anyway. The case proceeded to trial where Neumann (P) was granted a directed verdict as Tuccio (D) failed to establish a prima facie case. Neumann (P) then filed a vexatious litigation complaint against Tuccio (D). Tuccio (D) filed a special defense of advice of counsel. Neumann (P) then filed a motion to disqualify Tuccio's (D) attorney, John Williams, and the law firm John R. Williams and Associates, LLC (the "law firm").

ISSUE: Must a necessary witness have relevant and material testimony unobtainable elsewhere?

HOLDING AND DECISION: (Shaban, J.) Yes. A necessary witness must have relevant and material testimony unobtainable elsewhere. Connecticut's Rules of Professional Conduct address disqualification of party counsel. Rule 3.7 notes the proper action for an attorney who reasonably foresees he will be called as a witness is to withdraw. If the attorney does not withdraw, the court can disqualify him or her. The relevant inquiry is whether the attorney is a necessary witness. The defense of advice of counsel is of central importance in a vexatious litigation case and Neumann (P) needed to elicit the strategy and discussions between Tuccio (D) and Williams. Tuccio (D) argued the testimony was obtainable elsewhere because he could testify to the discussions, but that is unpersuasive. Tuccio (D) could not relay the same depth of information, analysis and advice because of the expertise an attorney has over a lay witness. Williams's testimony is both relevant and necessary, so he may be disqualified from representing Tuccio (D). Tuccio (D) argued the disqualification would work substantial hardship on the client, which is an excep-

tion for Rule 3.7 (i.e. Rule 3.7(a)(3)). Neumann (P) did not delay in filing the motion to disqualify and it was Tuccio's (D) choice to delay in raising the special defense. He brought on his own hardship. The motion to disqualify Williams is granted. The disqualification, however, is not imputed to the law firm. Neumann (P) has not shown a conflict between Tuccio's (D) position and the law firm's responsibilities to another client or its own position. The motion to disqualify the law firm is denied.

▶ **ANALYSIS**

Most states do not permit an attorney to advocate at a trial in which he or she is a necessary witness. Some states, however, do not compel disqualification if the movant fails to show prejudice arising out of the attorney-witness's dual role. In most instances, the attorney should withdraw from representation when being a witness is a likely possibility. Another attorney at the witness attorney's firm can step in as the advocate.

■▬■

Quicknotes

DISQUALIFICATION A determination of unfitness or ineligibility.

■▬■

Professional Regulation

Quick Reference Rules of Law

Cardillo v. Bloomfield 206 Corp.

Attorney (P) v. Contract beneficiary (D)

N.J. Super. Ct., 988 A.2d 136 (2010).

NATURE OF CASE: Appeal of decision invalidating attorney agreement.

FACT SUMMARY: Cardillo (P) simultaneously negotiated the Cardillo agreement restricting her private practice and the Rubinstein litigation settlement with the same parties. She later wanted to sue the Cardillo agreement beneficiaries, so she filed suit to declare the Cardillo agreement void and unenforceable.

RULE OF LAW
An attorney cannot offer or make an agreement to limit his or her private practice as part of a settlement of a controversy between private parties.

FACTS: Cathy C. Cardillo (P) represented Liberty Realty, LLC (Liberty), the three principals of which were Joseph Covello, James Stathis (D), and Steven Silverman (D). Stathis (D) and Silverman (D) also owned Bloomfield 206 Corp. (Bloomfield) (D). Cardillo (P) filed a lawsuit against Bloomfield (D) on behalf of her clients, the Rubinsteins (the "Rubinstein litigation"). Bloomfield (D) filed a motion to disqualify Cardillo (P) because of her prior representation of Liberty. While that motion was pending, Cardillo (P) began negotiating a settlement of the Rubinstein litigation. Simultaneously, Cardillo (P), Bloomfield (D), Stathis (D), and Silverman (D) negotiated an agreement wherein Cardillo (P) would agree not to represent parties adverse to defendants (the "Cardillo agreement"). Cardillo (P) and defendants' attorney exchanged emails in which they confirmed the Rubinstein settlement and the Cardillo agreement were separate issues being negotiated separately. On August 28, 2007, the parties executed the settlement agreement in the Rubinstein litigation. On August 29, 2007, the parties executed the Cardillo agreement. The Cardillo agreement limited Cardillo's (P) practice and defendants waived any conflicts of interest that may have arisen during the Rubinstein litigation. Defendants also agreed to withdraw any action asserting such a conflict. In January 2009, Cadillo (P) filed a lawsuit seeking injunctive relief finding the Cardillo agreement void and unenforceable as a violation of RPC 5.6(b) limited her private practice as part of a settlement of a controversy between private parties. Cardillo (P) wanted to represent a party in litigation against a corporation owned by Stathis (D) and Silverman (D).

ISSUE: Can an attorney offer or make an agreement to limit his or her private practice as part of a settlement of a controversy between private parties?

HOLDING AND DECISION: (Chambers, J.) No. An attorney cannot offer or make an agreement to limit his or her private practice as part of a settlement of a controversy between private parties. RPC 5.6(b) prohibits an attorney from offering or making an agreement in which the private practice is limited as part of a settlement. Such agreements restrict access to lawyers, may provide clients with rewards that are closer to buying off plaintiff's counsel, and create a conflict of interest with the interests of present clients and those of potential future clients. There is a strong public policy favoring the public's unfettered choice of counsel. Defendants argued the two agreements were separate as evidenced by the emails between Cardillo (P) and opposing counsel. This argument ignores the fact the two agreements were negotiated simultaneously and were intertwined. The Cardillo agreement is expressly related to the Rubinstein litigation because the defendants waived any conflict brought on by Cardillo's (P) representation of the Rubinsteins. The Cardillo agreement restricts Cardillo's (P) right to practice law and was part of the settlement of the Rubinstein litigation. It violates RPC 5.6(b) and is void and unenforceable. Affirmed.

ANALYSIS

It is not only an ethical violation to enter into a practice-restrictive agreement as part of a settlement, but it is a violation for an attorney to encourage another attorney to enter into such an agreement. Some attorneys have been disciplined for accepting cash in exchange for limiting private practice. Other attorneys have been disciplined for agreeing to in-house counsel requirements never to be adverse to the client corporation in unrelated matters. It is in an attorney's best interests to obtain and abide by an unrelated conflict waiver and maintain availability to represent future clients.

Quicknotes

CONFLICT OF INTEREST Refers to ethical problems that arise, or may be anticipated to arise, between an attorney and his client if the interests of the attorney, another client or a third-party conflict with those of the present client.

Florida Bar v. Went For It, Inc.

State bar (D) v. Lawyer referral service (P)

515 U.S. 618 (1995).

NATURE OF CASE: Grant of certiorari to determine constitutionality of specific attorney advertising practices.

FACT SUMMARY: A Florida lawyer and his lawyer referral service, Went For It, Inc. (P), challenged a Florida statute that prohibited personal-injury attorneys from sending direct-mail solicitations to victims and their relatives for thirty days following an accident as unconstitutional.

🏛 RULE OF LAW
A state may regulate direct-mail solicitations to potential clients if there is a substantial state interest that is directly and materially advanced by the statute and the statute is narrowly drawn to achieve that interest.

FACTS: A Florida lawyer and his lawyer referral service, Went For It, Inc. (P), challenged a Florida statute that prohibited personal-injury attorneys from sending direct-mail solicitations to victims and their relatives for thirty days following an accident as unconstitutional.

ISSUE: May a state regulate direct-mail solicitations to potential clients if there is a substantial state interest that is directly and materially advanced by the statute and the statute is narrowly drawn to achieve that interest?

HOLDING AND DECISION: (O'Connor, J.) Yes. A state may regulate direct-mail solicitations to potential clients if there is a substantial state interest that is directly and materially advanced by the statute and the statute is narrowly drawn to achieve that interest. While lawyer advertising is commercial speech entitled to First Amendment protection, such protection is not absolute. Intermediate scrutiny analysis is applied to restrictions on commercial speech. The state may regulate commercial speech that relates to unlawful activity or that is misleading. Speech that does not fall into either of those categories may be regulated if: (1) there is a substantial government interest being asserted; (2) the state shows that the restriction directly and materially advances that interest; and (3) the regulation is narrowly drawn. The Florida Bar (D) asserts a substantial interest in protecting the privacy of accident victims and their families against intrusive, unsolicited contact by attorneys, consistent with its objective of restricting activities negatively affecting the administration of justice. This Court has consistently held that this is a substantial state interest. Next, the state must show that the regulation directly and materially advances this interest. Here the Florida Bar (D) introduced a 106-page summary

of its two-year study on the effects of attorney advertising and solicitation, containing statistical and anecdotal data supporting its argument that such intrusions constitute violations of privacy and reflect negatively on the profession as a whole. Third, it must be determined whether the statute was narrowly drawn to further the state interest. This requires a reasonable fit between the legislature's goals and the means chosen to accomplish such goals. The thirty-day restriction is a reasonable means of achieving the state's interest. Reversed.

DISSENT: (Kennedy, J.) The advertising attorneys are merely communicating a willingness to help potential plaintiffs, which is constitutionally protected speech. Attorneys can educate the unsophisticated, uninformed client of her legal rights and potential claim which levels the playing field with more sophisticated parties who have access to information and representation. This cannot be considered mere commercial speech when the information conveyed transcends the self-interests of the speaker. The time limit is censorship and serves no legitimate purpose. If a person is offended by the communication, that person need not hire the advertising attorney. It is ironic that the Court now limits commercial speech of its own profession merely to avoid public criticism.

▶ ANALYSIS

The Court distinguishes the present case from its decision in *Shapero v. Kentucky Bar Association*, 486 U.S. 466 (1988), relied upon by the lower court in striking down the statute. There the statute in question imposed an absolute ban on attorney direct-mail advertising, without asserting a substantial state interest or any evidence in support of such interest. The Court rejected such absolute bans on attorney advertising without any empirical evidence of actual harm caused by such advertising.

■==■

Quicknotes

COMMERCIAL SPEECH Any speech that proposes a commercial transaction, or promotes products or services.

■==■

Campbell v. Asbury Automotive, Inc.

Class representative (P) v. Car dealer (D)

Ark Sup. Ct., 318 S.W.3d 21, 2011 Ark. 157 (2011).

NATURE OF CASE: Appeal from summary judgment in unauthorized practice of law action.

FACT SUMMARY: Campbell (P), as the class-action plaintiff representative, alleged Asbury Automotive Inc.'s (D) completion of a vehicle installment contract for customers constituted the unauthorized practice of law. Campbell (P) also alleged the retention of the document fee charged to complete the contract violated the Arkansas Deceptive Trade Practices Act.

🏛 RULE OF LAW
The legislature can provide a cause of action for a nonlawyer's unauthorized practice of law as long as the legislation in no way hinders, interferes with, restricts, or frustrates the powers of the judiciary to define, regulate, and control the practice of law.

FACTS: Asbury Automotive, Inc. (Asbury) (D) charged customers, including Campbell (P), a documentation fee for the completion of a vehicle installment contract. Campbell (P) filed a class-action lawsuit alleging the documentation completion for a fee constituted the unauthorized practice of law and the retention of the fee violated the Arkansas Deceptive Trade Practices Act (ADTPA). The trial court granted summary judgment. [The parties filed cross-appealed.]

ISSUE: Can the legislature provide a cause of action for a nonlawyer's unauthorized practice of law as long as the legislation in no way hinders, interferes with, restricts, or frustrates the powers of the judiciary to define, regulate, and control the practice of law?

HOLDING AND DECISION: (Danielson, J.) Yes. The legislature can provide a cause of action for a nonlawyer's unauthorized practice of law as long as the legislation in no way hinders, interferes with, restricts, or frustrates the powers of the judiciary to define, regulate, and control the practice of law. In *Preston v. Stoops*, 285 S.W.3d 606 (Ark. 2008), this court held ADTPA did not apply to the unauthorized practice of law by an attorney because the court holds the exclusive jurisdiction over the practice of law by attorneys. Here, however, this is the allegedly unauthorized practice of law by a nonlawyer. Statutes relating to the practice of law are in addition to the power of the judicial department and do not frustrate the power of the courts. The power of the judicial department to regulate the practice of law is "exclusive and supreme" but nonlawyers practicing law are beyond the purview of the court for purposes of meaningful sanction. The trial court erred in granting summary judgment. Asbury (D) asserted its completion of standard, pre-printed forms did not require the training, skill, or judgment of an attorney and it was not providing legal services or giving legal advice or counsel. This court previously noted many activities constitute the practice of law. Some, however, are permitted activities because it is in the public interest to permit limited, outside use of standard, printed forms. Standing alone, the completion of the forms is within the practice of law, but is a permitted exception. Asbury's (D) completion of forms did not comply with permitted, narrow exceptions and it charged a fee for the completion. The case law does not prohibit Asbury (D) from completing the forms as a service to customers, but it does prohibit Asbury (D) from collecting a fee for doing so. The court did not err in granting summary judgment to Campbell (P). Asbury (D) next argued there is no fiduciary relationship created because it cannot be held to the same standard as a practicing attorney. When one improperly assumes the function of a lawyer, the standard of care is that of a licensed attorney. The court did not err in so concluding. Reversed in part; affirmed in part.

DISSENT: (Brown, J.) This court alone regulates practicing lawyers, including out-of-state attorneys unlicensed in Arkansas, while nonlawyers shall not be so regulated. *Stoops* and *Born* [*Born v. Buchan Hosto, PLLC*, 2010 Ark. 292, 2010 WL 2431063 (2010)], manifestly prohibit a legislative foray into the practice of law.

▶ ANALYSIS

Each state's highest court regulates the practice of lawyers within its state. Some states permit nonlawyers to charge a document fee for certain transactions while others do not. Attorneys and laypersons should evaluate the relevant state law prior to charging anyone for completion of a legally binding document.

Birbrower, Montalbano, Condon & Frank P.C. v. Superior Court

(D/Petitioner), unlicensed in California v. Court (Respondent);

Corporation (P/Real Party in Interest)

Cal. Sup. Ct., 7 Cal. 4th 119, 949 P.2d 1, *cert. denied*, 525 U.S. 920 (1998).

NATURE OF CASE: Appeal from judgment that law firm practiced law without a license and was therefore not entitled to collect under fee agreement.

FACT SUMMARY: Birbrower, Montalbano, Condon & Frank P.C. (Birbrower) (D/Petitioner), a New York law firm unlicensed to practice law in California, performed legal services for ESQ (P/Real Party in Interest), a California-based corporation, without a license. ESQ (P) refused to pay, alleging malpractice and claiming that the firm could not collect its fee because of its unauthorized practice of law. Birbrower (D) counterclaimed for its fee.

RULE OF LAW

Advising a client and negotiating a settlement agreement without a license to practice law constitutes the unauthorized practice of law and no fee may be collected to the extent that the fee was for those services.

FACTS: ESQ (P/Real Party in Interest), a California corporation, retained Birbrower, Montalbano, Condon & Frank P.C. (Birbrower) (D/Petitioner), a New York law firm. None of the firm's attorneys were licensed to practice law in California. The fee agreement was negotiated and executed in New York, but provided that California law would govern all matters related to the representation. During several trips to California, the Birbrower (D) attorneys met with ESQ (P) and its accountants, gave legal advice, and made recommendations. They also spoke on their client's behalf during settlement agreement negotiations. ESQ (P) alleged malpractice, and Birbrower (D), counterclaimed to recover its fee.

ISSUE: Does advising a client and negotiating a settlement agreement without a license to practice law constitute the unauthorized practice of law such that no fee may be collected to the extent that the fee was for those services?

HOLDING AND DECISION: (Chin, J.) Yes. Advising a client and negotiating a settlement agreement in California without a license to practice law constitutes the unauthorized practice of law and no fee may be collected to the extent that the fee was for those services. The court then turned to the question of the meaning of "in California," holding that an unlicensed lawyer must engage in quantitatively sufficient activities within California or create a continuing attorney-client relationship for it to be determined that the attorney "practiced law in California." Although physical presence within the state is a factor, the court did not include that as a requirement in its analysis.

Ruling that Birbrower's (D) actions constituted the extensive practice of law in California, the court declined to permit the firm from collecting its fee to the extent that the fee was based on any of the work it performed while in California. Affirmed in part and reversed in part.

▶ ANALYSIS

The court recognized the distinction between the out-of-state litigator who obtains permission from a California judge to appear before that court pro hac vice and the out-of-state nonlitigator who cannot obtain similar authority to draft a legal document or provide legal advice to a client. Because case law offered no remedy for the nonlitigator who does not appear in a courtroom, the California legislature subsequently passed a law that permits, in effect, arbitrators the authority to admit out-of-state lawyers pro hac vice for in-state arbitrations.

Quicknotes

PRO HAC VICE Applicable to a specific occasion; the use or application of a condition for the limited duration of a single situation.

Judicial Ethics

Quick Reference Rules of Law

Cheney v. United States District Court for the District of Columbia

United States Vice President (D) v. Federal court (P)

541 U.S. 913 (2004).

NATURE OF CASE: Motion to recuse Supreme Court justice.

FACT SUMMARY: Justice Scalia attended a hunting trip at which Vice President Richard Cheney (D) was also present. Cheney (D) was the named defendant in a suit in which the Sierra Club was a plaintiff and which was granted certiorari by the Supreme Court. The Sierra Club moved to request that Justice Scalia recuse himself on the basis of the appearance of impropriety after the trip.

🏛 RULE OF LAW

The existence of friendship between a judge and a party to a pending case before the judge is not a basis for recusal when the named party is only nominally named in his official capacity.

FACTS: Justice Scalia attends a hunting camp in Louisiana each December-January recess of the Supreme Court. The camp is hosted by a friend who owns an oil rig services and parts company. Scalia extended an invitation to Vice President Richard Cheney (D) to attend the camp. Cheney (D) accepted and offered seats on his Government plane to Scalia, Scalia's son-in-law, and Scalia's son. Cheney (D) is required to fly on the Government plane for reasons of national security. Subsequent to the invitations and acceptances, the Sierra Club filed a writ of certiorari before the Supreme Court in which Cheney (D) was named in his official capacity as Vice President of the United States and head of a government committee. The Supreme Court granted certiorari. The men subsequently flew to Louisiana, attended the camp with other hunters, and Cheney (D) returned to Washington, D.C., after two days while the rest stayed on for several days and flew home commercially. The American press was outraged by the hunting trip and many newspapers published scathing editorials, replete with inaccuracies and misleading statements, demanding Scalia's recusal. The Sierra Club filed a motion to recuse based in large part on the editorials and the appearance of impropriety.

ISSUE: Is the existence of friendship between a judge and a party to a pending case before the judge a basis for recusal when the named party is only nominally named in his official capacity?

HOLDING AND DECISION: (Scalia, J.) No. The existence of friendship between a judge and a party to a pending case before the judge is not a basis for recusal when the named party is only nominally named in his official capacity. Impartiality can reasonably be questioned

when a friend of a justice is a party named in his personal capacity and that party's fortune or freedom is at issue. Here, despite the Sierra Club's protestations to the contrary, Cheney's (D) reputation and integrity are not at all at issue. The filed appeal requires the Supreme Court's consideration of a rather "run-of-the-mill legal dispute about an administrative decision." Further, social courtesies extended by government officials to justices have not previously been thought prohibited. Many justices accept dinners at the White House, which would be worth much more than a private flight on a government plane to Louisiana. The Sierra Club also fails to cite to relevant or persuasive legal authority for their argument to recuse. The majority of its motion is based on newspaper editorials. It is appalling to think that negative press could influence a Supreme Court justice to recuse when no legal basis for recusal exists. The recusal inquiry requires consideration by a reasonable observer informed of all surrounding facts and circumstances, not consideration of a biased editorial filled with inaccuracies. Examples do exist, however, of similar circumstances where recusal was not deemed appropriate. Justice White and Robert Kennedy vacationed together just prior to Robert Kennedy, as Attorney General, arguing a case before the Supreme Court vital to his brother's administration. Justice Jackson frequently socialized with Franklin Roosevelt before one of the most important Commerce Clause cases in history was argued. Socialization and friendship between justices and the executive branch and Congress has never been prohibited and should not be now. It is disheartening that the public might fear a Supreme Court Justice can be bought by nothing more than a flight on a government plane to go hunting with a friend. It would have been easier to recuse and not face the barrage of negative criticism, but recusal is simply not required here. Motion denied.

▸ ANALYSIS

The American press had a heyday with the Cheney-Scalia hunting trip (ignoring all of the other participants at the camp). Scalia's unprecedented, scathing memorandum opinion demonstrated his distaste for American media and his hope that the American public had more faith in the legal system and the Supreme Court. Critics of the memorandum, such as Lawrence J. Fox, read the memorandum as defensive, slightly ridiculous, and vintage Justice Scalia. Judges may have a duty to recuse from a pending case based on an appearance of impropriety, but the issue becomes the appearance to whom? The parties

Continued on next page.

involved? The public? Other judges? Justice Scalia points out that recusal at the lower court level has less of an impact on a case than recusal at the Supreme Court level because another judge is simply assigned to take the place of the recused judge. At the Supreme Court level, the lost judge is a lost vote, which could result in a tie and a prejudiced petitioner. Recusal is a fact-intensive inquiry.

■══■

Quicknotes

CERTIORARI A discretionary writ issued by a superior court to an inferior court in order to review the lower court's decisions; the Supreme Court's writ ordering such review.

■══■

Caperton v. A.T. Massey Coal Company, Inc.

Business owner (P) v. Coal company (D)

556 U.S. 868 (2009).

NATURE OF CASE: Appeal from reversal of jury verdict for plaintiff in state tort action on grounds that failure of one of the reversing justices to recuse himself was an unconstitutional denial of due process.

FACT SUMMARY: A jury rendered a $50 million verdict against A.T. Massey Coal Company, Inc. and its affiliates (collectively, Massey) (D). Thereafter, the state was to hold its judicial elections. Massey's (D) chairman, Blankenship, became the largest contributor to Brent Benjamin's campaign for election to the state's highest court, and Benjamin was elected by a slim margin. Before the state's highest court was to hear the appeal in the case, Caperton and his affiliates (collectively, Caperton) (P) asked Benjamin to recuse himself based on the conflict caused by Blankenship's campaign involvement, but Benjamin refused, and continued to do so repeatedly. The state's highest court reversed the verdict. Caperton (P) asserted that Benjamin's failure to recuse himself was a due process violation.

🏛 RULE OF LAW
Due process requires recusal of an elected judge where the judge is deciding a case involving the interests of a contributor, who by far made the largest financial contribution to the judge's election campaign and otherwise played a pivotal role in getting the judge elected, thus creating a "probability of bias."

FACTS: After a West Virginia jury found A.T. Massey Coal Company, Inc., a coal company, and its affiliates (collectively, Massey) (D), liable for fraudulent misrepresentation, concealment, and tortious interference with existing contractual relations and awarded Caperton, a business owner, and his affiliates (collectively, Caperton) (P) $50 million in damages, West Virginia held its 2004 judicial elections. The trial court denied Massey's (D) post-trial motions challenging the verdict and the damages award, finding that Massey (D) had intentionally acted in utter disregard of Caperton's (P) rights and ultimately destroyed Caperton's (P) businesses because, after conducting cost-benefit analyses, Massey (D) concluded it was in its financial interest to do so. Knowing the state's highest court, the West Virginia Supreme Court of Appeals, would consider the appeal, Blankenship, Massey's (D) chairman and principal officer, supported Brent Benjamin rather than the incumbent justice seeking reelection. Blankenship's $3 million in contributions exceeded the total amount spent by all other Benjamin supporters and by Benjamin's own committee. Benjamin won by fewer than 50,000 votes. Before Massey (D) filed its appeal, Caperton (P) moved to disqualify now-Justice Benjamin under the

Due Process Clause and the state's Code of Judicial Conduct, based on the conflict caused by Blankenship's campaign involvement. Justice Benjamin denied the motion, indicating that he found nothing showing bias for or against any litigant. The state's Supreme Court then reversed the $50 million verdict. During the rehearing process, Justice Benjamin refused twice more to recuse himself, and the court once again reversed the jury verdict. Four months later, Justice Benjamin filed a concurring opinion, defending the court's opinion and his recusal decision. The U.S. Supreme Court granted certiorari.

ISSUE: Does due process require recusal of an elected judge where the judge is deciding a case involving the interests of a contributor, who by far made the largest financial contribution to the judge's election campaign and otherwise played a pivotal role in getting the judge elected thus creating a "probability of bias"?

HOLDING AND DECISION: (Kennedy, J.) Yes. Due process requires recusal of an elected judge where the judge is deciding a case involving the interests of a contributor who by far made the largest financial contribution to the judge's election campaign and otherwise played a pivotal role in getting the judge elected, thus creating a "probability of bias." The Due Process Clause incorporated the common-law rule requiring recusal when a judge has "a direct, personal, substantial, pecuniary interest" in a case. In addition, there are other instances, as an objective matter, which require recusal where "the probability of actual bias on the part of the judge or decisionmaker is too high to be constitutionally tolerable." One instance involved local tribunals in which a judge had a financial interest in a case's outcome that was less than what would have been considered personal or direct at common law. Another involved a state supreme court justice who cast the deciding vote upholding a punitive damages award while he was the lead plaintiff in a nearly identical suit pending in the state's lower courts. The proper constitutional inquiry was not "whether in fact [the justice] was influenced," but "whether sitting on [that] case ... 'would offer a possible temptation to the average ... judge to ... lead him not to hold the balance nice, clear and true.'" Still another instance emerged in the criminal contempt context, where a judge had no pecuniary interest in the case but had determined in an earlier proceeding whether criminal charges should be brought and then proceeded to try and convict the petitioners. In this regard, the Court has said that "no man can be a judge in his own case," and "no man is permitted to try cases where he has an interest in the outcome." The judge's prior rela-

Continued on next page.

tionship with the defendant, as well as the information acquired from the prior proceeding, was critical. In reiterating that the rule that "a defendant in criminal contempt proceedings should be [tried] before a judge other than the one reviled by the contemnor," the Court noted that the objective inquiry is not whether the judge is actually biased, but whether the average judge in his position is likely to be neutral or there is an unconstitutional "potential for bias." Because the objective standards implementing the Due Process Clause do not require proof of actual bias Justice Benjamin's subjective findings of impartiality and propriety are not questioned, and there is no need to determine whether there was actual bias. Rather, the question is whether, "under a realistic appraisal of psychological tendencies and human weakness," the interest "poses such a risk of actual bias or prejudgment that the practice must be forbidden if the guarantee of due process is to be adequately implemented." Applying these principles here, there is a serious risk of actual bias when a person with a personal stake in a particular case had a significant and disproportionate influence in placing the judge on the case by raising funds or directing the judge's election campaign when the case was pending or imminent. The proper inquiry centers on the contribution's relative size in comparison to the total amount contributed to the campaign, the total amount spent in the election, and the apparent effect of the contribution on the outcome. It is not whether the contributions were a necessary and sufficient cause of Benjamin's victory. In an election decided by fewer than 50,000 votes, Blankenship's campaign contributions—compared to the total amount contributed to the campaign, as well as the total amount spent in the election—had a significant and disproportionate influence on the outcome. The risk that Blankenship's influence engendered actual bias is sufficiently substantial that it "must be forbidden if the guarantee of due process is to be adequately implemented." The temporal relationship between the campaign contributions, the justice's election, and the pendency of the case is also critical, for it was reasonably foreseeable that the pending case would be before the newly elected justice. The fear of bias arises in such a situation when—without the other parties' consent—a man seems to choose the judge in his own cause. Applying this principle to the judicial election process, there was here a serious, objective risk of actual bias that required Justice Benjamin's recusal. In other words, on these extreme facts, the probability of actual bias rises to an unconstitutional level. Massey (D) is mistaken in predicting that this decision will lead to adverse consequences ranging from a flood of recusal motions to unnecessary interference with judicial elections. The case at bar presents an extraordinary situation whose circumstances are extreme by any measure, and, because the States may have codes of conduct with more rigorous recusal standards than due process requires, most recusal disputes will be resolved without resort to the Constitution, making the constitutional standard's application rare. Reversed and remanded.

DISSENT: (Roberts, C.J.) The majority's decision will undermine—not promote—impartiality on the bench. The majority's "probability of bias" standard is too undefined to provide adequate guidance as to when recusal is constitutionally mandated, which will inevitably lead to an increase in allegations that judges are biased, however groundless those charges may be. Despite the majority's repeated emphasis on the need for an "objective" standard, the standard announced by the majority is too vague to be objective. Even if the majority is correct that the case at bar is extreme, it does not follow that claims of judicial bias will not be brought to test the "probability of bias" standard, since claims that have little chance of success are nonetheless frequently filed. Regardless of their merits, such claims will inevitably bring the accused judge, and the judicial system as a whole, into disrepute. Moreover, it is not at all clear that the case at bar is, in fact, an extreme case. Blankenship's contributions were overwhelmingly independent contributions over which Benjamin had no control, and there were many other indications that Benjamin's election had nothing to do with Blankenship's contributions, but rather was influenced by his opponent's gaffes, newspaper endorsements, and other factors (other than contributions) that normally affect elections.

▶ *ANALYSIS*

In *Caperton,* the Court seemingly rejected the well-established appearances-based recusal standard in favor of a probability-based standard that examines the likelihood of actual bias. The appearances-based standard is employed by the federal recusal statutes as well as state judicial codes of conduct, and the issue before the Court was whether appearance of bias alone can rise to the level of a due process violation. Some courts—and Justice Benjamin himself—have taken the position that due process does not require recusal based on the appearance of bias alone, and that due process is implicated only where actual bias is shown. Others have taken the position that mere appearance of bias can violate due process, and some take the position that "appearance of bias" and "probability of bias" are synonymous. By adopting the "probability of bias" standard, the majority arguably was aiming to avoid constitutionalizing the appearances-of-bias standard and to create an objective test based on the likelihood that a reasonable judge would actually be biased under a particular set of circumstances.

■▬■

Quicknotes

BIAS Predisposition; preconception; refers to the tendency of a judge to favor or disfavor a particular party.

Continued on next page.

DUE PROCESS The constitutional mandate requiring the courts to protect and enforce individuals' rights and liberties consistent with prevailing principles of fairness and justice and prohibiting the federal and state governments from such activities that deprive its citizens of life, liberty, or property interest.

RECUSAL Procedure whereby a judge is disqualified from hearing a case either on his own behalf, or on the objection of a party, due to some bias or interest on the part of the judge in the subject matter of the suit.

Glossary

Common Latin Words and Phrases Encountered in the Law

A FORTIORI: Because one fact exists or has been proven, therefore a second fact that is related to the first fact must also exist.

A PRIORI: From the cause to the effect. A term of logic used to denote that when one generally accepted truth is shown to be a cause, another particular effect must necessarily follow.

AB INITIO: From the beginning; a condition which has existed throughout, as in a marriage which was void ab initio.

ACTUS REUS: The wrongful act; in criminal law, such action sufficient to trigger criminal liability.

AD VALOREM: According to value; an ad valorem tax is imposed upon an item located within the taxing jurisdiction calculated by the value of such item.

AMICUS CURIAE: Friend of the court. Its most common usage takes the form of an amicus curiae brief, filed by a person who is not a party to an action but is nonetheless allowed to offer an argument supporting his legal interests.

ARGUENDO: In arguing. A statement, possibly hypothetical, made for the purpose of argument, is one made arguendo.

BILL QUIA TIMET: A bill to quiet title (establish ownership) to real property.

BONA FIDE: True, honest, or genuine. May refer to a person's legal position based on good faith or lacking notice of fraud (such as a bona fide purchaser for value) or to the authenticity of a particular document (such as a bona fide last will and testament).

CAUSA MORTIS: With approaching death in mind. A gift causa mortis is a gift given by a party who feels certain that death is imminent.

CAVEAT EMPTOR: Let the buyer beware. This maxim is reflected in the rule of law that a buyer purchases at his own risk because it is his responsibility to examine, judge, test, and otherwise inspect what he is buying.

CERTIORARI: A writ of review. Petitions for review of a case by the United States Supreme Court are most often done by means of a writ of certiorari.

CONTRA: On the other hand. Opposite. Contrary to.

CORAM NOBIS: Before us; writs of error directed to the court that originally rendered the judgment.

CORAM VOBIS: Before you; writs of error directed by an appellate court to a lower court to correct a factual error.

CORPUS DELICTI: The body of the crime; the requisite elements of a crime amounting to objective proof that a crime has been committed.

CUM TESTAMENTO ANNEXO, ADMINISTRATOR (ADMINISTRATOR C.T.A.): With will annexed; an administrator c.t.a. settles an estate pursuant to a will in which he is not appointed.

DE BONIS NON, ADMINISTRATOR (ADMINISTRATOR D.B.N.): Of goods not administered; an administrator d.b.n. settles a partially settled estate.

DE FACTO: In fact; in reality; actually. Existing in fact but not officially approved or engendered.

DE JURE: By right; lawful. Describes a condition that is legitimate "as a matter of law," in contrast to the term "de facto," which connotes something existing in fact but not legally sanctioned or authorized. For example, de facto segregation refers to segregation brought about by housing patterns, etc., whereas de jure segregation refers to segregation created by law.

DE MINIMIS: Of minimal importance; insignificant; a trifle; not worth bothering about.

DE NOVO: Anew; a second time; afresh. A trial de novo is a new trial held at the appellate level as if the case originated there and the trial at a lower level had not taken place.

DICTA: Generally used as an abbreviated form of obiter dicta, a term describing those portions of a judicial opinion incidental or not necessary to resolution of the specific question before the court. Such nonessential statements and remarks are not considered to be binding precedent.

DUCES TECUM: Refers to a particular type of writ or subpoena requesting a party or organization to produce certain documents in their possession.

EN BANC: Full bench. Where a court sits with all justices present rather than the usual quorum.

EX PARTE: For one side or one party only. An ex parte proceeding is one undertaken for the benefit of only one party, without notice to, or an appearance by, an adverse party.

EX POST FACTO: After the fact. An ex post facto law is a law that retroactively changes the consequences of a prior act.

EX REL.: Abbreviated form of the term "ex relatione," meaning upon relation or information. When the state brings an action in which it has no interest against an individual at the instigation of one who has a private interest in the matter.

FORUM NON CONVENIENS: Inconvenient forum. Although a court may have jurisdiction over the case, the action should be tried in a more conveniently located court, one to which parties and witnesses may more easily travel, for example.

GUARDIAN AD LITEM: A guardian of an infant as to litigation, appointed to represent the infant and pursue his/her rights.

HABEAS CORPUS: You have the body. The modern writ of habeas corpus is a writ directing that a person (body) being detained (such as a prisoner) be brought before the court so that the legality of his detention can be judicially ascertained.

IN CAMERA: In private, in chambers. When a hearing is held before a judge in his chambers or when all spectators are excluded from the courtroom.

IN FORMA PAUPERIS: In the manner of a pauper. A party who proceeds in forma pauperis because of his poverty is one who is allowed to bring suit without liability for costs.

INFRA: Below, under. A word referring the reader to a later part of a book. (The opposite of supra.)

IN LOCO PARENTIS: In the place of a parent.

IN PARI DELICTO: Equally wrong; a court of equity will not grant requested relief to an applicant who is in pari delicto, or as much at fault in the transactions giving rise to the controversy as is the opponent of the applicant.

IN PARI MATERIA: On like subject matter or upon the same matter. Statutes relating to the same person or things are said to be in pari materia. It is a general rule of statutory construction that such statutes should be construed together, i.e., looked at as if they together constituted one law.

IN PERSONAM: Against the person. Jurisdiction over the person of an individual.

IN RE: In the matter of. Used to designate a proceeding involving an estate or other property.

IN REM: A term that signifies an action against the res, or thing. An action in rem is basically one that is taken directly against property, as distinguished from an action in personam, i.e., against the person.

INTER ALIA: Among other things. Used to show that the whole of a statement, pleading, list, statute, etc., has not been set forth in its entirety.

INTER PARTES: Between the parties. May refer to contracts, conveyances or other transactions having legal significance.

INTER VIVOS: Between the living. An inter vivos gift is a gift made by a living grantor, as distinguished from bequests contained in a will, which pass upon the death of the testator.

IPSO FACTO: By the mere fact itself.

JUS: Law or the entire body of law.

LEX LOCI: The law of the place; the notion that the rights of parties to a legal proceeding are governed by the law of the place where those rights arose.

MALUM IN SE: Evil or wrong in and of itself; inherently wrong. This term describes an act that is wrong by its very nature, as opposed to one which would not be wrong but for the fact that there is a specific legal prohibition against it (malum prohibitum).

MALUM PROHIBITUM: Wrong because prohibited, but not inherently evil. Used to describe something that is wrong because it is expressly forbidden by law but that is not in and of itself evil, e.g., speeding.

MANDAMUS: We command. A writ directing an official to take a certain action.

MENS REA: A guilty mind; a criminal intent. A term used to signify the mental state that accompanies a crime or other prohibited act. Some crimes require only a general mens rea (general intent to do the prohibited act), but others, like assault with intent to murder, require the existence of a specific mens rea.

MODUS OPERANDI: Method of operating; generally refers to the manner or style of a criminal in committing crimes, admissible in appropriate cases as evidence of the identity of a defendant.

NEXUS: A connection to.

NISI PRIUS: A court of first impression. A nisi prius court is one where issues of fact are tried before a judge or jury.

N.O.V. (NON OBSTANTE VEREDICTO): Notwithstanding the verdict. A judgment n.o.v. is a judgment given in favor of one party despite the fact that a verdict was returned in favor of the other party, the justification being that the verdict either had no reasonable support in fact or was contrary to law.

NUNC PRO TUNC: Now for then. This phrase refers to actions that may be taken and will then have full retroactive effect.

PENDENTE LITE: Pending the suit; pending litigation under way.

PER CAPITA: By head; beneficiaries of an estate, if they take in equal shares, take per capita.

PER CURIAM: By the court; signifies an opinion ostensibly written "by the whole court" and with no identified author.

PER SE: By itself, in itself; inherently.

PER STIRPES: By representation. Used primarily in the law of wills to describe the method of distribution where a person, generally because of death, is unable to take that which is left to him by the will of another, and therefore his heirs divide such property between them rather than take under the will individually.

PRIMA FACIE: On its face, at first sight. A prima facie case is one that is sufficient on its face, meaning that the evidence supporting it is adequate to establish the case until contradicted or overcome by other evidence.

PRO TANTO: For so much; as far as it goes. Often used in eminent domain cases when a property owner receives partial payment for his land without prejudice to his right to bring suit for the full amount he claims his land to be worth.

QUANTUM MERUIT: As much as he deserves. Refers to recovery based on the doctrine of unjust enrichment in those cases in which a party has rendered valuable services or furnished materials that were accepted and enjoyed by another under circumstances that would reasonably notify the recipient that the rendering party expected to be paid. In essence, the law implies a contract to pay the reasonable value of the services or materials furnished.

QUASI: Almost like; as if; nearly. This term is essentially used to signify that one subject or thing is almost analogous to another but that material differences between them do exist. For example, a quasi-criminal proceeding is one that is not strictly criminal but shares enough of the same characteristics to require some of the same safeguards (e.g., procedural due process must be followed in a parole hearing).

QUID PRO QUO: Something for something. In contract law, the consideration, something of value, passed between the parties to render the contract binding.

RES GESTAE: Things done; in evidence law, this principle justifies the admission of a statement that would otherwise be hearsay when it is made so closely to the event in question as to be said to be a part of it, or with such spontaneity as not to have the possibility of falsehood.

RES IPSA LOQUITUR: The thing speaks for itself. This doctrine gives rise to a rebuttable presumption of negligence when the instrumentality causing the injury was within the exclusive control of the defendant, and the injury was one that does not normally occur unless a person has been negligent.

RES JUDICATA: A matter adjudged. Doctrine which provides that once a court of competent jurisdiction has rendered a final judgment or decree on the merits, that judgment or decree is conclusive upon the parties to the case and prevents them from engaging in any other litigation on the points and issues determined therein.

RESPONDEAT SUPERIOR: Let the master reply. This doctrine holds the master liable for the wrongful acts of his servant (or the principal for his agent) in those cases in which the servant (or agent) was acting within the scope of his authority at the time of the injury.

STARE DECISIS: To stand by or adhere to that which has been decided. The common law doctrine of stare decisis attempts to give security and certainty to the law by following the policy that once a principle of law as applicable to a certain set of facts has been set forth in a decision, it forms a precedent which will subsequently be followed, even though a different decision might be made were it the first time the question had arisen. Of course, stare decisis is not an inviolable principle and is departed from in instances where there is good cause (e.g., considerations of public policy led the Supreme Court to disregard prior decisions sanctioning segregation).

SUPRA: Above. A word referring a reader to an earlier part of a book.

ULTRA VIRES: Beyond the power. This phrase is most commonly used to refer to actions taken by a corporation that are beyond the power or legal authority of the corporation.

Addendum of French Derivatives

IN PAIS: Not pursuant to legal proceedings.

CHATTEL: Tangible personal property.

CY PRES: Doctrine permitting courts to apply trust funds to purposes not expressed in the trust but necessary to carry out the settlor's intent.

PER AUTRE VIE: For another's life; during another's life. In property law, an estate may be granted that will terminate upon the death of someone other than the grantee.

PROFIT A PRENDRE: A license to remove minerals or other produce from land.

VOIR DIRE: Process of questioning jurors as to their predispositions about the case or parties to a proceeding in order to identify those jurors displaying bias or prejudice.

Casenote® Legal Briefs